Modern Worship

Lowell Institute Lectures 1927

Modern Worship

BY VON OGDEN VOGT

New Haven : Yale University Press

LONDON · HUMPHREY MILFORD

OXFORD UNIVERSITY PRESS

1927

MGE

To my Wife

PREFACE

FOUR *of the chapters herewith presented are the Lowell Institute Lectures for 1927, on the Form and Content of Modern Worship. They are printed as read excepting that the third lecture had to be somewhat curtailed in the reading. The additional chapter contains some brief comments on aspects of worship which need attention today. There is a considerable desire for larger quantities of concrete materials which can be worked up into services of worship, but they simply do not yet exist. Experiments are being made and new materials formulated, but not on a sufficient scale or of sufficient merit for publication as suitable for widespread adoption. The time should soon be here, however, for such a collection. I have not attempted to coördinate the theory of worship here set forth with other major conceptions, but rather for the sake of simplicity and clarity to keep within the limits of the suggestion of worship as celebration. That others are thinking along similar lines is indicated by a few excerpts from two papers in* The International Journal of Ethics *for July, 1926, from* Sperry's Reality in Worship, *Pratt's* Religious Consciousness *and* Wieman's Religious Experience and Scientific Method.

VON OGDEN VOGT.

The First Unitarian Church,
   Chicago, Illinois,
      July 26, 1927

CONTENTS

I. Religion as Celebration   I

Celebration in ordinary life. Character of celebration as enjoyment and recollection. The festal character of historic religion.
The vitality of form. The relation of celebration to truth, to
ethics, and to the beauty of life. The changing recollective content of worship. The object celebrated.

II. Liturgical Form   29

The laws of form in all the arts. Study of unity, movement,
rhythm, style, design. Application of aesthetic canons to the art of
liturgics. The principal patterns of worship.

III. Liturgical Materials   55

The liturgical revival. Dilemma of old and new content. Illustrative materials for the several elements of worship: Preparation,
Presentation, Humility, Vitality, Recollection, Illumination, Dedication, Peace.

IV. The Aesthetics of Structure   105

The unifying value of structure. Rhythm, movement, color, proportion, style, materials, surface and mass. Significance of the
altar. Intimations of human presence. The external building as
symbol. Recollective symbols; traditional, educative, industrial.

V. Problems in Contrast   131

Formality and informality. Subjective and objective. Enrichment
and simplicity. Specific and generic religion. Personal and social
religion. Congregational participation and priestly conduct.

Index   155

CHAPTER I

Religion As Celebration

Worship is like a breathing spell in a long and arduous foot race, or the hour of roll call in a prolonged and hard-fought battle: . . . it is altogether indispensable to sane and wholesome living—it is important enough in life to warrant the erection of classical temples and Gothic cathedrals. It is indeed so important that one finds one's self sometimes wondering how any of us can afford to do anything but educate ourselves in this art. . . . To be effectively a person and thereby help others to be persons is the sum of the abiding satisfactions of life. Worship in the sense of this aim is natural and necessary, and in the Great Community all mature men worship. Its objectives are not absolutely fixed as to their content.

GUY ALLAN TAWNEY

I.

OUR first thoughts together will remark some of the relations of form and content in worship considered under the aspect of celebration. The second lecture will discuss the place of form in worship by a brief note of the formal elements in any work of art, whether pictorial, structural, musical or other, and the application of the findings to the particular art of worship. The third lecture will offer some definite suggestions of concrete material for the different parts of the liturgy, some specific content for modern worship. The fourth and last lecture will seek to discover the formal values and content possibilities to be developed not through the liturgy but by the church building, its structural forms and the symbolisms of its decoration.

There are many ways of approaching the problem of worship, some of them of great value and suggestiveness. For the sake of simplicity and clearness I am proposing abruptly to consider worship as the celebration of life. For the sake, also, of the so-called religious outsider, I put the matter thus. There are many modern men and women of high spiritual gifts who do not find themselves at home in any of the households of specific faith. Some of these are scientists and thinkers, some philanthropists, while others find their spiritual happiness in the world of the arts. The religious institution is itself in great measure responsible for the alienation of many of her choicest children. It has so often defined religion in terms of particular ideas or ideals that many of those who could not agree with its definition have been lost to mother church. Yet I do not hesitate to challenge the intelligence of the outsider, to criticize his way of life and to commiserate his truncated and partial experience. It can still be claimed for the public worship of the church that it offers the one incomparable privilege and opportunity for the all-comprehending expression of the life of man. The cause of social welfare beomes barren without some vision of what is to be the beautiful content of that welfare. The arts cannot come to maturity without a robust humanism. Philanthropy and art need each other and the place to meet is at the celebration of life which rejoices in both. As to the thinker, modern religion does not ask his agreement to any intellectual tenets whatever. It would say, rather, Take all your thoughts and all your experiences of life, roll them together, think them together and enjoy them in the highest and purest way. Religion includes definitions and deeds, but first of all it is celebration. It is time to turn the tables upon those who ignore religion. They have too long assumed that the God of religion was an abstraction, a weakly held postulate, an impossible assumption. But the God whom we seek in the worship of today is the great reality, whatever its nature be. We are not bent upon any inconsequential exercise or any fool's errand, but upon that high and perpetual quest in comparison with which every other mode of life is indeed an abstraction. There is that beyond ourselves, yet embracing ourselves, with which we have to deal

and which will deal with us. Religion is the attempt
to understand that relation, which is an actual one,
and to enjoy it. Primarily, the religious moment is
not the moment of action or of thinking but the moment of joy. Historically, the worship of man is most
accurately characterized not as intellectual or moral
but as festal.

Celebration is a prominent aspect of ordinary life.
In the nation's life, special holidays are set apart for
the remembrance of founders and heroes, victories
and deliverances and other aspects of national or civic
good fortune. The old-fashioned agricultural fair
and the new-fashioned industrial exhibit, together
with the occasional larger exposition, constitute celebrations of the resources of the land and the achievements of toil. Much of the charm of domestic life
centers about intimate family celebrations. A man
gets a raise in pay, and takes his wife out to dinner,
just for a little celebration. Birth and wedding anni-
versaries are made occasions of festivity. Public holidays are customary opportunities for the heightened
realization of family and personal connections. The
great religious holidays contribute a powerful tone to
the spiritual temper of a people. In these celebrations, life is perpetually readjusted to its principal
centers of reference. They are not composed merely
of the trivialities of light pleasure, but often rise to
the quality of an august measurement of time and
the significance of events and of persons.

The celebration is an occasion of vivid recollection.
It remembers again the original event which has be-

come important in the life of persons or of nations. The celebrations of a people thus become at length the description of its philosophy of life, the definition of those things which are most highly valued. Yet the celebration is also an occasion of vivid present enjoyment. The past event is recalled and celebrated not from a sense of duty but largely as an opportunity for a new festival occasion. Sometimes the original significance of the event celebrated is all but lost in the perpetuation of the custom for its own sake. This leads to the multiplication of insignificant and unworthy celebrations, which very fact is ample testimony to the prevailing desire for life as it is realized in celebration. If people are so prone to unworthy festivals how much more might they be led to those which are highest and purest.

There is a moment familiar to all men, frequently achieved by many men, a moment of unconscious celebration. It is the moment of rest after toil, of review and satisfaction, of well-being and quiet singing happiness. It is very close to the heart of the religious experience. The laborer comes home from the mill or the mine with his pay check at the close of the week. He buys food and shoes and all things needful for his home and children. When all is provided and all are fed, he sits with his pipe in the evening of the day, profoundly happy that he has been able to be a good provider, profoundly thankful for the generous providence in which he finds his well-being. I have seen this in other men and I know it myself. In the strange and sweet notes of a flute sounding from the housetop through the Egyptian twilight, I have heard the immemorial pain and desire and ecstasy of man. This is the inner praise and celebration of life which is religion. It is the acknowledgment of grace and the assumption of responsibility. To lift this experience into consciousness and universality is the nature and function of public worship. To be in love with life, to have a zest for life, to find it good, to love not merely this or that partial good, but to love life, all of it, to love God, this is religion. To praise and celebrate life, not merely this good fortune or delivery from that distress, but the memory of all things, the hope of all things, life entire and complete, to praise God and to celebrate his goodness, this is worship.

Celebration is on the whole the most prominent aspect of historic religion. Our own spiritual lineage derives from a definite historic religion, the religion of the Old Testament, and we have not yet exhausted its rich intimations. A more complete study, covering the usages of other faiths, would display some of the same results, but we are most familiar with those of our own inheritance. Through several hundred years of Jewish history, the practical meaning of religion to the tribesman was the celebration of the great feasts. I do not say that it did not mean many other things also, local rites and family usages, great thoughts and revolutionary teachings, regulations and habits become almost second nature in the midst of daily life, and all the long and intricate story of the rise and fall of its customs. But from the beginning of the national history until the destruction of the temple at Jerusalem by Titus, the distinctively religious experience of the common people was centered about the great cultural festivals of the year, the feast of unleavened bread, the feast of weeks, the feast of the passover. Before the legal reform of Deuteronomy the rites and ceremonies of the tribal high places constituted a rich apparatus of popular festivity. After the reform the major daily sacrifices of the temple at Jerusalem were essentially cultural and festal. No more evidence than that of the eighth-century prophets themselves is needed to reveal the chief features of the national religion and its popularity. Feasts of the new moon and solemn assemblies, unmoral and perhaps immoral, were loved and cherished by the people. It is very difficult for Protestants, with our intense intellectual interest in religion, and our convinced identification of moral earnestness with religion, to imagine popular religion so absorbingly festival in character as was the actual religion of the Jewish kingdoms.

The essential nature and power of the religious experience for them was its high enjoyment. Probably no great cult was ever developed because it was consciously considered enjoyable. Probably no great cult was ever developed without a differing mixture of motives on the part of those concerned with it. Some essential basis of genuine belief in the practical efficacy of the rite was doubtless at the heart of every religious usage. But this does not tell the whole story. Certainly the king fostered the cult, as kings have al-

ways done, in part at least because of some recognition of its power as an agency of control and its force
for societal cohesion. Surely the high priest, standing
beside the king, shared a variation of the same motive. Still another variation of non-religious motivation, possibly more mixed with earthly elements,
doubtless influenced the common priest. And the
people themselves, if they were taught to perform
the prescribed rites in order to retain the favor of the
Lord of Hosts in time of war, or the local gods of
fertility in time of peace, actually did maintain them
because they enjoyed it. If they were taught that they
could secure divine favor for the arms of the nation
and the harvests of the year, what they really wanted
was something better, and what they got was something better, a season of celebration, release from
drudgery, high festivity with their kinsfolk and
friends, and some stir of noble companionship as
tribes before the Lord. I do not say that they got
these things in their highest or purest forms. I do say
that what they got without a conscious motive for
seeking it, a by-product, so to speak, of what they
were supposed to get, was really the most valid thing
in their experience. I am putting the matter in this
way partly because I have recently heard it said that
the rites of religion were always developed to secure
what man needed, victory in war and the harvests of
peace, and that now no rites are required because man
can supply his own necessities. But what man has always desired and needed and now desires is not the
divine assistance for fat harvests, but the divine com-

munion for its own sake as the highest happiness and destiny.

It is important to distinguish in the history of popular religion between assigned motives and real motives. Religious acts have always been performed for some reason clear to consciousness, taught and received through tradition, but also out of urgencies less clearly defined, half-instinctive, possibly half-debased, yet also in part more true to essential realities and more near to the highest values than the specified purposes themselves. If the king fostered the cult for one reason, though he proclaimed another, and so also the high priest and the common priest, each real reason differing from each specified reason, the common people did the same. They attended on their religious duties in part because they believed what they were taught of the values to be derived. I am myself convinced that they attended to their religious duties in the main because they enjoyed it.

A candid analysis of Christian history will disclose no different conclusion. In the whole history of Christian worship, many other urgencies have been effective, fear, discipline, duty, ambition, the dire necessities of sorrow, the despairs of sin and all the manifold complexities which enter into the motivation of human conduct. But on the whole, Christians have always gone to church and still go to church because they enjoy it. Mediaeval religion was not all fear of hell nor Puritan religion all conscience, and as for Wesleyan religion, it developed an almost riotous pleasure in the religious revival. It would be necessary to review the whole brilliant pageantry of the Catholic centuries to gain any adequate impression of the festal character of Christian worship throughout the most of its history. In certain countries today there is still maintained an elaborate system of feast days and ceremonial occasions which are the opportunities of celebration for the people. Yet nowhere can be found anything like the amplitude of the full mediaeval development which undoubtedly carried to inordinate excesses the celebrative side of life. I do not pretend to claim that Protestantism has displayed much conscious interest in religion as celebration. I do believe that Protestant human beings, like other human beings, have maintained their services of religion in the main because of the high happiness of the religious experience realized in public worship. As Protestants we like to believe that our religious loyalties are based upon great convictions and the manly assumption of moral responsibilities, and I have no quarrel with this wholesome point of view. I am only seeking to suggest that the moment of worship is a time for the legitimate enjoyment of those convictions, and an occasion for the incomparable satisfactions of the highest self-realization by the renewal of loyalties. There may always be differences of opinion concerning the endless chains of causes and effects, the perpetual and unbroken linkages of means and ends. Possibly some will always regard as ends what others designate as means. There are dangers both ways. I simply choose to regard high communion as the end, thoughts and affairs as means. And I believe this choice, either consciously or unconsciously, to be that of the majority of religious people.

The celebrative side of religion may thus be called its central aspect. Religion has always had its mental interest, its cosmogonies, its philosophies, its theologies. It has always had its moral interest, its divinations, its lawgivings, its prophecies, its personal and social reforms. But these are not religion itself. They describe it or issue from it. They are assisting causes, or resultant activities, or only abstractions, not the complete and living experience. The great annual festival, the feast-day, the holiday, the weekly service of worship, these have fostered religion itself, these have been the immemorial occasions of the fullest life.

The celebrations of religion revive and recall not simply one event or a single hero nor even the history and political fortune of a whole people, but all events, all peoples, all conceptions, all of life. Religion celebrates nothing less than the whole of man's existence and all his faiths about its source, nature, duties and destiny. Worship is essentially the praise and celebration of life. In worship, man comes before the Lord with psalms and hymns and spiritual songs. As in all celebration, the religious festival is not merely the barren recollection of a good that once was. It is present joy and power, the happiness of an immediate touch of life at its highest and best.

This is the abiding element in religion. Ideas

change, theologies come and go, but the celebration of life remains. Morals change and ethics are redefined, but their ends are not in themselves. Something more vital and comprehensive, that abundant life that is desired by all, and for all, must have some occasion of actualization. Here is our first glimpse of the relation of form and content in religion. The great generic mold of celebration is the abiding form of religion. The often replaced mass of ideas and ideals is the ever changing content. The one is necessary for identity and reference, the other for growth and development. The one gives joy and vitality, the other genuineness and direction. The one is penetration to the heart of things, the other regard for the farthest orbits of existence.

Our first suggestion, then, is that there is much in common life and in the history of specific religion to favor the conception of worship as celebration.

Meanwhile, we have reached a field of problems. If religion is the celebration of faiths, what about error? If religion is the celebration of life as good, what about evil? If religion is celebration in the beauty of the holy day, what about the ugliness of many other days? Before an answer to these questions is attempted, however, it is necessary to make one more comment about the form of worship. That comment is this, that it is primarily the form of worship rather than its content which is the chief source of the vitality of the experience and hence of its high enjoyment.

I well know the objections which will be directed

against such a proposition, that you cannot have religion that does not seek to be true, nor religion that is not founded upon righteousness. With both of these assertions we must all agree, but they cannot gainsay the findings of a study of the psychological facts. Let me admit here a real danger of our times. There is a renewed interest in the forms of worship which is becoming widespread. There is an increased interest in all the arts which is reflected in the revolutionary improvement in church building taking place today. There is a revival of the minor ecclesiastical arts such as would be extremely shocking to the early Puritans if they could see it. I fear the dangers of this movement as much as anyone, the dangers of seeking directly those rewards which come only from dedication and sacrifice. I believe as much as anyone that we cannot have the greatest worship without great convictions, that we cannot have the greatest worship without a sweeping, searching moral passion on the part of earnest leaders, possibly not without the enkindling of a popular movement of moral idealism. Only the great periods of formation and re-formation in faith and morals have established long continuing norms of public worship. The norms have not been mere shapes, they have been forms fashioned in part at least by great faiths and consuming ethics. But there are several further things to say. One is that we do not at just this time have the pleasure of living at a moment of widespread agreement concerning the ideas and the ideals of life which compose the content of worship. If we are to have worship at all just now, we must have it in a less pervasive way than the popular adherences of such large-scale movements as Lutheranism, Puritanism or Wesleyanism in their initial stages. For another thing, it is possible that we may be ourselves upon the eve of a comparable reformation. We have already at hand many of the materials which are to fashion the faiths and the ethics of the coming time. Amongst the new materials which are at hand those which belong in the region of the arts cannot be ignored. It is obviously necessary to discover and use the findings of science that are significant for religion. It is also necessary to appraise the revival of the arts and discover the validities which it contains. Again, the major forms of normal worship cannot be changed every year or two, nor every generation or two, merely to fit all the passing fashions in ideas and ideals. Genuinely revolutionary ideas do not come so frequently nor do ordinary persons experience frequent revolutions in character. The normal values of worship are found in its power to quicken and revive generally accepted conceptions. Furthermore, there are many of us who hold that the normal forms of worship follow a psychological pattern rather than an intellectual or moral one, as I shall hope to discuss later. These considerations answer most of the objections against the proposal that the vitality of the experience of worship is derived more largely from form than from content.

Still the objector may not be satisfied. Do you mean to say, he asks, that a sense of the peace of God is a derivation of some outer formal physical influence rather than of the spirit? I do mean to say something very like that, and the same concerning other religious feelings. In unusual situations, some disaster, some swirling confusion of events, or other crisis drives the spirit to seek sanctuary and peace. In the round of ordinary life, the spirit does not rise to the capacity of great apprehensions without a precedent stir of the senses by some space or shape or sound, formal in character.

In support of the proposition of the derivation of vitality from form, I ask you to note the facts of your own experience or observation, the immediate appeal of form to the senses, and the deliberate use of form to vivify content. In ordinary celebration there is usually some material element cast in such a form as to express and vivify the festival. It may be a birthday cake, it may be a grand civic parade, but the occasion is hardly a celebration without it. It is probably true ordinarily that more people go to church for good rhetoric than for new ideas. There are of course times and circumstances when a whole community or a whole nation are moved by the stir of new thoughts. Yet if in the midst of just such times our proposition is true, how much more is it true in less critical times. There are hundreds of preachers in America today teaching the same ideas that Dr. Fosdick does, who do not have so many hearers. Quite simply, he is a superior artist in rhetoric. It may be said that there are today multitudes of people mentally restless, spiritually unsatisfied, milling round, hunting round for some truth to guide them, seeking light. So there are, perhaps more than ever before. Yet it might be said with more truth that what they are seeking is abundant life. They will never find a neat little package of ideas to satisfy them, but they may be led to find a rich and beautiful life. I have a neighbor and friend, an excellent preacher, an entirely genuine and sweet-spirited man, who likes to think that people come to hear his ideas. To some extent he is correct. Yet he has a curiously charming gift of poetic speech, and once admitted to me that he thought people came again because they got some little lift from that quality. I remind you, moreover, of the considerable number of notable preachers, whose ideas have been commonplace, if not shoddy, some of whose morals have been weak if not low, who have drawn multitudes of hearers by the gift of tongues. I think often with most grateful remembrance of the very beautiful white meeting house in the Connecticut hills where first I preached. The parishioners were mostly farmers. It is a profound gratification to feel that during a ministry of several years amongst those admirable people, there was a real progress in the truth. Yet I am convinced that the most of them came to church because there they received, through the inspiration of the various forms utilized, a revival of faiths and a renewal of courage for the duties of life. Simply to change their workaday clothes and sit in even rows together in the old white meeting house was a formal habit alone sufficient to make the difference between civilized life and barbarism. If all this be true in these instances of religious bodies supposed to be little influenced by form, how much more must it be true amongst those bodies where the formal arts, structural, plastic, pictorial and ceremonial, have been more extensively developed. I do believe that many times whole religious bodies or whole movements of religious interest have been stirred by the sheer spiritual appeal of new thoughts and new moral outlooks. But I believe also that ordinarily the religious imagination has been moved to activity and to high enjoyment by the formal elements of the great cultural ceremonies. This is generally true of Old Testament religion, of Christianity and, indeed, of the history of all religions.

It is true because of the direct immediate appeal of good form to the senses. The formal elements of worship do not need any intermediaries. They are themselves the words, the communicating agencies, the mediators between God and man. The effects of form are immediate and physical. Then the effects of the effects are imaginative and spiritual. New peace and fresh courage doubtless come from new insights of faith or new realizations of truth. But usually the insights of faith are enabled by the increased vitality which is the gift of some kind of form. And as for realization, it is realization, not just reality conceived or defined, but reality touched, tasted, mixed with. Realization is partly physical, a profound relation of form and content in which the harmony of form is always present.

Moreover, forms in worship have always been used to vivify ideas and to rekindle ideals. They are vehicles of truth, vessels of communication, channels of deliverance. They have served not only as direct appeals to the senses, assisting the mind to develop its own thoughts, but also as symbols for the conveyance of thoughts. The idea without form is a timid tapping that does not rouse the sleepy householder; clad in good form it blows a bugle at the gates of the soul. Religion has always used abstract forms, proportions, shapes, colors, sounds, for the direct appeal to the senses. It has also set forth definite conceptions clothed in many kinds of symbolic form.

These considerations are sufficient to indicate the meaning of the second of our suggestions, that in popular worship it is the formal element rather than the content which is chiefly the source of the vitality and the enjoyment of worship.

Celebration is at once recollection and present joy. The content equipment of the celebrant is the whole structure of his ideas and the whole fabric of his toil recollected. These are brought together into harmony, significance and worth in a moment of totality and realization. That realization is assisted by the formal modes devised to present it. All things are brought and offered and lost in the whole, there to be found again for what they are. The fruits of toil are devoted and eaten, so to speak, by the god and the god gives new fruition. All paths lead to the high joy of communion, and by the life and power of that communion any path may be ventured. Worship is the interruption of work to celebrate. Celebration is achieved in forms of praise and festivity and communion. The celebration of life, the praise of God, requires the most elevated of forms to be in harmony with the lofty character of the content. In that praise and that communion which constitute good worship are engendered the powers necessary for the renewal of good works.

We should now be prepared to return to the questions already raised about error and evil and ugliness if worship is to be regarded as the celebration of life.

Respecting the question of truth and error, the immediate answer is that no other conception of worship so frees us from the dilemma of an ever changing mental content. To begin with, the thing celebrated is life itself, whole, complete, unlimited, not merely knowledge of life, not merely speculations about life, yet certainly not excluding either knowledge or speculation. The celebration of life attempts to include all things. The celebrations of specific religion can least of all afford to be unmindful of error, not only the error of other faiths but the error inside its own faith. If in former times religion came declaring the finalities of its truth, today it comes admitting its intellectual incompleteness. There are many who find the essence of religion in their specific convictions, whose religious loyalty is a loyalty to certain conceptions. These have often regarded the celebrations of religion as lacking in loyalty to truth, whereas the facts of the situation are just contrariwise. Those to whom religion is bound up with specific truths cannot be so loyal to truth itself. A passion for the truth is a necessity in the celebration of life. It is not a necessity for lesser celebrations. No one can come before the altars of religion to celebrate life as a whole and there remember that the courts of truth have aught against him, without first becoming reconciled to the possibility of any revolutionizing conceptions whatsoever. The celebration of life means celebration of truth seeking rather than of particular truths, though I believe that more often than is done, the institutions of religion should develop occasions of rejoicing over the major increments of human knowledge.

Thus is overcome the antinomy of the heart and the head, of feeling and thinking. The religious cult, the festal ceremonies of religion have always been criticized for their unintellectual character. Today, no less than in former times, worship is set forth as subjective and hedonistic, as a delicious retreat from reality, unstable and shifting upon the ever uneasy sands of the emotions. It is accused of fascination and hypnosis, dulling the mental interest. If our study of the influence of form, however, means anything, its influence is precisely the opposite. By perverse and unworthy manipulation, forms may be used as enticements away from intellectual adventure. Left to itself, good form enhances vitality, enlarges the imagination and fits the mind for the exercise of its highest power.

The necessary intellectual assumptions of the religious festival are not extensive. They may be discovered to be profound and far-reaching in the hands of the philosopher and theologian whose business it is to deal with them. As artists in worship, it is not our special concern to say what they are. Our concern is to take the findings of the thinker and do the best we can with them. It is not primarily our task to specify the events, whether fateful or providential, whether divine or human, that are to be celebrated, nor to define the nature of the Object of our devotions. It is rather our task to lead the worshiper into the presence of reality, into the presence of God, however these ultimates may be conceived. I am unwilling to admit that worship is nullified by any conception of reality. I am willing to admit that some conceptions of existence render worship extremely difficult and make an almost superhuman demand upon the courage of man to sustain his life. The chief concern of the celebrant is that nothing be omitted. Religion is the all comprehending category, and worship cannot leave out of its account any of the great certitudes of the mind or any of the great possibilities of speculation. To suggest that man cannot worship at all or celebrate his life with high satisfaction unless committed to this or that particular conception of reality is to yield at once to unmitigated despair. On the other hand, to weave into his celebrations ever fresh formulations of truth is artistically a very difficult undertaking. But it is not an impossible undertaking, and there is no honorable escape from the charge of subjectivity and retreat if it be not attempted.

As to the question of good and evil, again the answer is involved in the all comprehending character of the celebration of life. How can life be praised and celebrated when life as a whole includes pain, darkness and cold, injustice and sin and wrong? If religion cannot afford to exclude the remembrance of error, much less can it forget the prevalence of evil. Just here is the brave and daring paradox of Christianity, that in the same breath it remembers evil and calls the remembrance the celebration of the Lord's supper. The chief rite of Christendom is a recollection of tragedy, but the man who conducts it is not referred to as the president or the chairman but as the celebrant.

When a Christian betakes himself to worship, at the very heart of his faith is a symbol of the worst that man could do to his brother man. The central celebration of Christianity plunges at once to the dregs. It remembers not brightness and good fortune but defeat and disaster. With magnificent courage it determines to ignore nothing, but to face all the facts, including the worst facts of human existence. He celebrates life as a whole not because it is all good, but because much of it is good and he is determined to make good of the rest. The Eucharist is a great celebration because it is a great sacrament of dedication. The central symbol of Christianity is not a reminder of the kindly forces of nature nor the normal fortunes of man but of defeat turned into victory, of pain transformed into benefit, of evil overcome with good. If there is a permanent validation of the cross, and a mighty wholesome health in its retention amongst the symbols of religion, it is its unceasing demand for facing all the facts of life, its perpetual call to ignore nothing, its glorious assertion that happiness is possible, yet not possible without righteousness and high purpose and good will. Indeed, perhaps the Christian is the only one who can celebrate life, precisely because he does celebrate all of it.

Thus is overcome the antinomy of faith and works, culture and morals. The festival, the celebration, the religious cult, has always been accused of unmorality, of enjoyment without righteousness. But if the religious celebration upgathers into itself the recollection of the practical life, including all that needs correction or reform, the vitality which it engenders not only assists in the comprehension of the right but also supplies energy to perform it.

Those phases of life which are celebrated because they are good and the evils of life which need correction because they are bad need from time to time new definition. Into the great abiding forms of the celebration must be put the ever changing content of the moral situation. Protestantism has of course always had and will continue to have the sermon as the great vehicle of moral urgence and in so far as the sermon is included in the apparatus of worship it assists in the perpetual process of stimulating ethical thought and purpose. Yet Protestantism has not yet succeeded in giving sufficient recognition to ethics in its devotions, in its worship more properly so called. The prayers of Dr. Rauschenbusch, some new litanies of labor and other experiments have been made. These efforts to specify the ever changing moral content of religion need to be pursued with greater variety and intensity. I shall hope to make later one or two definite suggestions for the symbolic teaching of ethics possible to the church of the future.

There remains the question of beauty and ugliness, which like the others finds its solution in the comprehensive character of worship. The celebration is itself a work of art, but the things it selects for remembrance and praise are the lovely things of common life. And because the memory of the religious celebration is exceeding long, it turns all nobility into beauty and declares that every life may be beautiful, transcending success and defeat.

Saul and Jonathan were lovely and pleasant in their lives, And in their death they were not divided:

Not divided from their beauty as well as from each other. In the communion of saints, there is beauty for each and all.

Thus is overcome the antinomy of retreat and association, of work and play. Festal religion has been accused of offering an anodyne, a false respite from the prevailing sordidness of life. In this criticism, of course, all the other arts must share as well as the art of worship. But what are the arts? Every normal man seems to be endowed with an indestructible urge of creativity, an unceasing desire for the establishment of the work of his hands. The arts have been defined by some as a field where man might more easily achieve creative success than in the rougher and less malleable stuff of industrial and political life. Yet here also the assumptions of worship are far-reaching. If, in the harmonies of worship, an ideal beauty of all things is envisioned, that harmony is a presage and promise of realization in actuality. Here also Protestantism needs new experiments in the way of artistic encouragement to this process of actualization. It should be possible in the celebrations of religion to give to men not an anodyne for the monotony of daily toil, but some clear comprehension of what it is that that daily toil contributes to the present necessities and the coming perfection of society, and to the transformation of all sordid things into a beautiful world.

In this connection, it must not be forgotten that a large proportion of men do not find their daily toil ugly or irksome. Not the least hearty of the celebrations that go on amongst us are those of commerce and industry. In my own city many of its inhabitants meet together frequently for the celebration of their commercial affairs. Their hearts are in their work and its achievements. It is almost their religion. All this commercial festivity should be brought inside the great frame of public worship, where its commendable qualities might be given recognition and sanction but where also its isolation and injustice might find the correction of a larger reference, wider outlook and purer motive.

The beauty of holiness is the beauty of that which is uncommon and sacred, discovered in retreat and sanctuary, but it is also the beauty of sharing toils and responsibilities in the associations of common and secular life. The desire for beauty, the impulse to make things beautiful is afforded range and opportunity to all men as they celebrate on holy days and as they do on other days that which is worthy of celebration.

If religion then be the celebration of life, it comprises and completes all kinds of goods, mental and moral and aesthetic, human and divine. It corrects the partiality of all categories, it is itself the comprehending category. Whatever a man celebrates is in a sense his religion, yet it is usually a very meager religion unless it rises to the qualities of the religious category so recognized. Celebration must be brought to consciousness and universality before it becomes true religion.

On the one hand, thinker and philanthropist and aesthete suffer shortage and lack without the fullness which is the celebration of all things. The many things of each need to be brought into association with the many things of the others. And not only that, for celebration is not merely the recollection of many good things, it is the discovery of the total significance of those things. It is the praise of that wholeness of life which they comprise, that One which alone is completely good. Worship as celebration is the great form of collectivity and of composition.

But worship, on the other hand, offers no fixed content of its own. Its content is all that is brought to it. What we desire as churchmen today is not to foist upon thinker or doer or artist any outworn concepts or projects defined by the past alone, but to fill the abiding form of our celebration with the new content of every man's good thoughts and good deeds.

Is this then the Object of worship, the stuff of common life? Is this God? No, not yet at least. One brings all his goods to the temple, but there is a door of leaving behind, where he must be rid of his many goods as he desires to be rid of his many bads, if he is to find the one supreme Good. Is the temple then stuffed with all his worldly goods? Yes, and with the goods of all other men, and the immeasurable goods that are where no man is. Here are the corded bales of every man's good and the shards and ashes of every man's bad. Here is all in the world that he has loved and all that he has ignored. He comes to be rid of the world and to find God. But here he finds all the world he has left behind—and behold! it is God.

CHAPTER II

Liturgical Form

Science, then, returns to art its stuff, criticized, corrected, and substantially bettered. This is precisely what modern theology should do for modern worship. The idea-substance of our services of worship should be far better for its criticism at the hand of the natural, the historical, the psychological, and the social sciences. Our present ineffectualness in worship, however, lies in our failure to reaffirm the temper and technique of the artist. We are too often content with a drastically criticized body of religious truth. We do not realize that this body of truth must be forever recreated in new, significant forms.

WILLARD L. SPERRY

II.

ASSUMING that worship is an art, it must have its technique of form as any other art. The limits of our time will not permit a defense of the assumption, nor a proper discussion of informal modes of worship, if indeed there can be such a thing as informal worship. Certainly good form in worship is often destroyed by informalities. Most of the objections to form in worship are due to misconceptions of form. It is our present purpose to study briefly the laws of form in the arts generally, and notice their application to the particular art of worship.

Undoubtedly, the first canon of the arts is singleness, wholeness, unity. Whatever is not composed into some kind of integrity is not a work of art. Whatever cannot be managed or relegated to a position of proper contribution must be omitted from the work of art. This does not mean that the several parts are to be overwhelmed by the dominating modes of unification. Yet no parts can be so much emphasized as to weaken the unity of the whole. Nor can greatly dissimilar parts be brought together in one work unless they are adequately subordinated in the scheme of the whole, as, for instance, the inclusion of both a formal garden and a wild tanglewood in the same landscape composition or the inclusion of read prayers and free prayers in the same service of worship. If the total design is sufficiently extensive, such opposites can be managed, though not in juxtaposition. Our chance illustration is as good a point as any from which to view the far-reaching implications of this canon of unity. The desire for unity is one of the most elemental of human desires, unity of self and unity in the world. There is a profound if simple pleasure in the easy apprehension of the unity of a porcelain bowl or a brief melody. That satisfaction is increased many fold by the apprehension of the comprehending unity which organizes into a single whole the many parts and intricate relations of a great symphony or a Gothic cathedral. The logic of this desire has no limits. It becomes at last the grand conviction that there is an ideal unity of all things, and the high moral purpose to realize it. How altogether necessary is this law of unity for the art of worship. Whatever disturbs the unity of liturgic form is essentially a moral disturbance. Whatever contributes to the unity of that form assists the apprehension of the ultimate union which is religion itself.

There are many artistic methods for achieving this quality of integrity and many ways of failing to achieve it. One of the most frequent disturbances of unity in worship is the personal intrusion of the minister, shifting the attention of the worshipers from the great Object to the physical setting of the time and place. There is a type of worship, the old-fashioned prayer meeting, where the personal direction of the leader is itself a mode of unification. Yet those whom I remember as most helpful leaders in such meetings were men who, when the climax of spiritual value was reached, offered their direction in most skillfully impersonal ways. In the normal public worship of the Sunday service, the minister should no more interpose a personal note than an actor should address a personal remark to the audience in the midst of a play. Another common break-up of unity is occasioned by a sudden change in the tone or style of a service, just as distracting as would be the telling of a story in two or three dialects.

In order to secure unity for the ordinary public service of worship, the parts of the service must each fall into its proper place in some total design, the movement must be uninterrupted, and some selected style or tone maintained. Oftentimes certain repetitive phrases or responses assist the unity of a liturgy in much the same way as the repetition of the same kind of arch or window in a building or the same color repeated in the furnishings of a drawing-room. It is of course obvious that unity in theme or content is necessary in worship as in any other art. This does not necessarily involve the inclusion of the sermon in the unity of the worship theme, though in general I believe it to be desirable. It is less obvious and not so easy to devise harmony between the form and the content. Forms suitable for the celebration of a football victory are not adequate for worship. Offenses against this requirement are far more frequent than they should be. A style of service does not need to be stilted or cold or artificial in order to be properly dignified and elevated in tone. We do not want any forms that are not the genuine expressions of a spirit. Such forms are formalistic. Forms are hollow mockeries unless they have been wrought out of profound

realities, needs and desires, convictions and joys. Yet
the great realities are only vivid for us as they are
bodied forth in great forms. In the highest art, form
and content are so wedded and welded into one that
both are essential to the expression, as, for instance,
in the twenty-third Psalm, the content could not exist
for us in the way it does without the incomparable
form which presents it. Without any attempt fully to
cover the methods and modes of unity, I suggest only
so much as an indication of its importance.

The next law of form in the arts is that of movement. The song, the dance, the drama, the novel,
these all move. A large proportion of works in the
pictorial and plastic arts indicate movement, and actually set up tendencies of motion in the physical organism of the beholder. It would seem that a service
of worship should move. It must not be a static but a
flowing thing. The primary movement is in the
hearts of the worshipers themselves. If the service
does not move them they must furnish the movement
themselves, and if there be no motion of the spirit
amongst the people, the service cannot move others.
Over the proscenium arch of one of our theaters is
inscribed the wholesome admonition: "You your-
selves must set flame to the fagots which you have
brought." But it is difficult for the worshiper to sustain the movement of worship if the forms of expression do not move with his experience. Many
services are not prepared to afford movement of expression. They have no inevitable sequence. They
reach forth to no climax. They constitute a series of

separate parts, not a flowing stream of vital life. Various kinds of things interrupt the movement of worship and their opposites sustain it. Awkwardness in following the service disturbs the movement. If, for instance, the people are standing for a hymn and are obliged to remain standing while finding their places for a reading, this is an ill-managed point in the service and breaks its continuity. Points of transition from one part to another are often abruptly made and check the movement. They may be smoothly made and add momentum to the service. An anthem presented without transitional preparation becomes a concert number. The same work preceded by preparatory versicles becomes the expression of the whole body of worshipers. Sometimes the organ by a brief graduating interlude can effect an important transition from one part to another. Especially lengthened parts tend to interrupt the flow of movement. Otherwise excellent music often does this, while a brief period of silence does not. Changes in the style of the material or the manner of its presentation interrupt the movement of worship. Only a certain discipline of coöperation between minister, choristers and congregation can develop and carry forward to its full cycle that grandeur of movement which is possible where there is a genuine desire for the highest worship.

Another almost universal element of form in the arts is that of rhythm, which is a form of actual or suggested motion. Poetry, music and dancing are essentially rhythmic arts. The colonnades or the fenestration of a noble building make a rhythmic appeal. Rhythm is one of the most exciting and hence enlivening influences. Antiphonal singing and responsive readings are primitive forms of rhythm, and are used in most services of worship largely for that reason. The processional march is valuable for its rhythmic effect. Far more profound and important than these primitive forms of rhythm is the larger rhythm of alternation in worship, the forth and back swing of the attention from the One to the many, from the self to God. This alternation should find ample opportunity of expression in the forms of the service. It is not an easy thing to accomplish, but unquestionably one of the necessities for adequate expression in worship. For the more quiet and intimate occasions of worship, it is naturally achieved by the simple direction of the service. For larger numbers of people, the personal method breaks the movement and hence the rhythm. For the full public service, forms are required which have larger carrying power. From one point of view, the whole service of worship is one of the great poles of the alternating life, the other being the workaday world. But as there may be worship in work so there must be a remembrance of work in worship. Those outer forms and usages in the service of worship which emphasize the interplay of life between these two great foci of the particular and the universal are of prime importance in the realization of these great relations.

The selection and development of style is one of the formal necessities in all the arts. Every utterance which has effective power of communication is composed in some distinctive style. The form of language in written or spoken address may be restrained or florid, prosaic or poetic, using the diction of the street or developing the more precious phraseology of the sophisticated. Out of the practical and cultural life of peoples as they have developed and reached maturity have come successively the great architectural styles. In the drama of the day we speak of certain presentations as being highly stylized. By a combined process of elimination and caricature, scenes and figures are set before us not in realistic but in significant form. Style thus emphasizes the dominating qualities of persons or of movements or of peoples. Style is never the product of weak or spineless character. In the lesser arts it represents personal distinction. In the grander arts it represents maturity and societal integration. In all the arts, style is one of the elements which sustains the aesthetic experience. It takes the mind out of its accustomed channels and preoccupations and prejudices and holds it aloof from these where its judgments may be exercised in the most free and untrammeled manner. It produces the artistic effect of distance by which alone life may be surveyed dispassionately. It takes us momentarily away from private and particular interests to a position where all things can be estimated without the warping concern for their personal bearings. It is one of the most perplexing of the formal problems of worship today. One of the very attitudes which worship is designed to accomplish is this achievement of

aloofness and freedom which the arts effect in part by
success of style. Our practical dilemma is the problem
of the old and the new in the content of worship. If
we use the thoughts of today in the language of every
day, how shall we achieve the necessary artistic distance, the desired religious elevation? If we retain
the higher tone of ancient utterances, how shall we
be true to our own thoughts and latest revelations? I
am convinced that the services of worship which do
not retain anything of the magnificent heritage of
devotional utterance from the past do not possess the
elevation of style necessary to call forth the experience of worship. The familiar and more or less ancient phraseology succeeds where newer and fresher
formulations fail. The reasons are simple. A form of
utterance which has become archaic conducts us im-
mediately away from the world of present interests
and images. It assists the process of elimination and
of withdrawal from the present time and place. It
swiftly cuts away the more obtruding impressions and
thus serves the process of concentration. Besides this,
it begins the positive process of religious imagination. It suggests images with which former religious
experience has been connected and reminds us that we
are called to worship a reality that has been operative
hitherto and that ever more shall be. The new formulations tend to occupy the mind with conceptions
and thus to obscure for the moment that larger comprehending mystic awareness and realization which is
worship itself. Yet many ancient formulations of
faith or devotional utterances are burdened with too

much out-worn intellectual content. If this is the case for particular worshipers, the sense effect of the utterance is nullified. A very practical problem of every minister is that of selecting from the materials of the past those treasures which are least burdened with abandoned concepts. There are of course those who would seem to be too easily offended by the content of ancient materials who need the general corrective of poetry for their overly prosaic temperament.

In a general way, the proper position for the older materials of worship and the archaic style is in the opening parts of the service. As the experience of worship moves on, it must return to the life of today, practical life and intellectual life and the whole mass of present interests and affairs. The service must make place for the actual concerns of people whatever their character. There are no ancient words to express all these concerns. They must be phrased in new formulations. Although the sermon is the best opportunity for this, the general service of worship will become remote and unreal if it does not also include some of these new elements. One of the hopeful signs of the day is the increasing tendency to introduce into services of worship suitable extra-Biblical materials. Only good taste and patient experiment can make this usage successful. Some churches use for responsive readings selections from modern moral and religious writings or material prepared by the minister himself. This is very difficult because the difference in style is usually noticeable and hence distracting. It is questionable also because the responsive reading is a rhythmic exercise used chiefly for its sense appeal and imaginative stimulus rather than because of its content value. A less difficult usage of new material is the introduction of a second or substitute scripture reading taken from modern sources. This will often give to a brief service a freshness that is both delightful and helpful. In some ways, also, an original litany comprised of a content of modern concerns, with brief responses by the people, is far less difficult from the point of view of the demands of style than the responsive reading. If there are those who desire for their religious meetings the expression of modern concepts only, they will find it very difficult to engage in worship at all. They may develop many interesting ideas, possibly true and important ideas, and many useful values in such a meeting, but they can hardly develop the distinctly religious experience, that withdrawal from the many which seeks to apprehend the One, that celebration of all things, that complete experience which is worship itself.

We must turn to a more complex element in all the arts, the element of design. Every work of art has some pattern or design, a major arrangement of space, a major marking off of time or sound, covering the entire extent of the work. The design may be a simple symmetry, as in a cup, or it may be composed of intricate patterns in more than one medium overlaid and interwoven, yet as a whole harmonized together. The dancers trace figures upon the floor, fashion innumerable designs in posture and weave intricate patterns of repetitive motion. Some paintings have a major design of color differing from, yet harmonious with, the design that is composed by the arrangement of the objects depicted. There might be said to be a pattern of comedy and a pattern of tragedy. A so-called grand opera is a composite design involving the lesser patterns of sound and color and movement woven into the grander dramatic design. Incidentally, what is called grand opera is often not successful in design. Sometimes the theme utilized is not worthy of the scale of pattern attempted. The resulting work may offer many charming parts but breaks down as a whole. The technician in the arts looks at once for the pattern. As a technician his interest in content is subordinated to his interest in design. The power of pattern is a manifold one. It is essential to the individuation of parts without which the work becomes barren. It is one of the main resources for developing unified experience and one of the major factors in sustaining the experience. The satisfaction in pattern merges into the desire to create patterns until at last nothing will be omitted from a total design of life. It is thus a symbol of totality, an immediate assistance to the apprehension of the oneness of all things.

What is the pattern of worship? How shall we discover the typical design which will compose and represent the experience we desire to express and so to reproduce for ourselves and others? Many answers have been made to this question, although not always under the form of the question of pattern. The sim-

plest of the worship designs is the twofold or bal-
anced pattern of initiation and response. According to
this view, God calls to man and man answers to God.
It conceives of worship as a real event in which there
is the actual initiating activity of God and the re-
sponding activity of man. The conception of worship
generally held amongst the Lutheran churches follows this simple and powerful description. Throughout the whole service of worship, in this Lutheran
view, there are two alternating elements, the sacramental and the sacrificial, the grace of God and the
offering of man. Always in the service, the action of
the minister is of this twofold order. Now he stands
for God before the people administering a sacrament.
Again he stands for the people before God offering a
sacrifice. The service is a kind of conversation between man and God. Some have elaborated this design by describing the episodes of the action of God
and by analyzing the elements of the response of
man according to the laws of attention. It is possible
that this account of worship is true and that no more
valid pattern of worship than this can be discovered.
Yet it is too simple to express sufficiently some of the
important elements in the experience.

Various tripartite patterns of worship have been
suggested. Professor Buckham[1] has indicated a pattern following closely the ancient categories of truth,
beauty and goodness. The three elements of worship
in his analysis are: The Direct Individual Experience
of Truth; The Culture of the Soul by Contempla-

[1] John Wright Buckham, *Religion as Experience*, p. 105.

tion; and The Dedication of the Self in Love. Certainly worship includes these great phases. Some will feel, however, that just this mode of arranging them does not follow the normal order of the experience of worship, and also that it is slightly confusing in its categorical outline. According to our view it is not truth but reality which is touched in the religious experience. The experience may be fostered by the presentation of statements of truth and in turn it may clarify the truth, but it is itself the apprehension of reality. Professor Buckham has elsewhere said the same thing. The pattern of worship suggested by Dean Sperry[1] is also a tripartite or triangular design. According to some of the terms he has used in describing it, it appears to be suggested by a philosophic interest in that it consists of thesis, antithesis and synthesis. As thesis, there is the Vision of Reality. The antithesis is the Contrasting Human Situation. These are resolved in a synthesis of New Comprehension, including Rededication. It will be observed at once that the elements of the experience here suggested are in general agreement with the other threefold pattern. Probably Professor Buckham would admit a sense of a contrasting human situation and new comprehension as a part of the cultivation of the spirit by contemplation. Both these patterns, however, make no reference at all to a phase of the experience which to my own mind is one of its most important aspects, its vitality. In other statements Dean Sperry has included it. But in this formal statement of the pattern

[1] Willard L. Sperry, *Reality in Worship*, p. 282.

of worship he has been obliged to omit one important matter and also to include two distinct elements in the third category in order to compress the description into this threefold form. Similar to these patterns is one suggested by Professor Brightman,[1] comprising Contemplation, Revelation, Communion and Fruition.

If the patterns of Buckham and Sperry have an intellectual cast of description, that of Hartshorne is derived from the moral interest. Dr. Hartshorne[2] suggests a clearly defined pattern of worship including five points. There is first, Review of what has taken place, either deliberate or forced; secondly, Attention to what might have taken place; thirdly, Re-evaluation of the past act by contrasting with the ideal and consequently regret that what might have been was not, accompanied by feelings of strain and estrangement; fourthly, if Regret, then Identification with the ideal, with the point of view of God, with a consequent sense of forgiveness or feeling of worth through this identification; fifthly, Recovery or Achievement of peace, release, sense of fellowship with God, unity with mankind, at-one-ness with the universe. Here are, in somewhat differing form, the same marks of the experience we are seeking to describe. To my thought, however, the normal experience begins by the turn of attention to the universal rather than to the particular. Human beings are often

[1] Edgar S. Brightman, *Religious Values*, pp. 180-184.
[2] Hugh Hartshorne, *Yale Divinity News*, Vol. XXII, No. 4, May, 1926.

driven to the search for God by their own mistakes and sins, that is, by the pressure of particulars. Yet even in critical situations it is some forgotten ideal remembered which calls attention to the mistake or wrong. In the more everyday experience of life, it is not so much the flagrant wrong as it is the lower good which needs correction, and this again is recognized as lower good only by the vision of some higher good. In addition to this, the pattern suggested by Dr. Hartshorne is not an easy one to follow in the order of service. It would be difficult to construct a service of worship composed of elements expressive of the several stages of experience as he has outlined them.

At this point it is necessary to state more explicitly a principle which we have been assuming in our brief introduction to the problem of design in the art of worship. The principle is this, that the outer form of the exercise of worship should parallel the inner order of the experience of worship. With this principle both Sperry and Hartshorne as well as others are in agreement. If the principle be a correct one the first task of the artist in worship is to analyze the experience. It may be opposed to this suggestion that there is no typical experience of worship, that the many varieties of religious experience cannot be reduced to one general norm. How can the good and the bad, the fortunate and the unfortunate, the souls at peace and the spirits distracted, the religious and the irreligious, find in any one pattern the solution for their situation? Without discussing the question, I only ex-

press my own view that in the main there is a comprehending normal experience which covers all these
major differences. However varied the situation of
the worshipers in mind, body or estate, however
varied the approaches, whether mental or emotional
or moral, the essential psychology of the experience
is identical.

In a previous discussion[1] I have suggested a five-
part pattern developing through the elements of
Vision, Humility, Vitality, Illumination and Dedication. I am now inclined to suggest a design of seven
elements, preceded by a kind of introduction or pro-
logue. In addition to this, may I remind you of the
suggestion made a moment since that sometimes in
the art of painting, a design composed of the arrangement of objects in space is overlaid by another design
formed by an arrangement of colors, or of light and
shadow. In somewhat analogous fashion this pattern
of elements in the experience of worship is overlaid
and harmonized with the ever present alternating
rhythm of attention to the One and the many which
is the principal character of the twofold pattern already noticed.

It is difficult to give expression in the formal liturgy to the problem of personal approach, although
many services begin in this way. Every service which
has a Call to Worship begins with the state of the
worshiper in mind rather than by a presentation of
divinity. This is one definite method of introduction
to worship. In the Roman missal the question of ap-

[1] *Art and Religion*, Chapter XV.

proach takes the form of an expressed purpose to worship,

I will go to the altar of God.

This note of expectancy and purpose is reëchoed throughout the first responsals in the Ordinary of the mass.

Send forth thy light and thy truth:
They have conducted me and brought me unto thy holy hill,
    and into thy tabernacles.
To thee, O God, my God, I will give praise upon the harp.
I will go in to the altar of God;
To God, who giveth joy to my youth.

In the Anglican liturgy the opening sentences are for the most part of this preparatory character, followed by the call to repentance and later by the Venite. The Unitarian hymnal services each contain an exhortation to worship. In all these and others, there is a notable recognition of this preparatory element and definite liturgical expression of the state of the worshiper in his approach toward God. I confess that I have not myself adopted any of these usages, nor found any other satisfactory method of taking this element into account. I submit it to your attention as a matter for thought and experiment, with one further question about it here. What can we do, either in the service of worship or by way of instruction concerning worship, to develop amongst religious people the attitude and practice of going to church not to hear or to receive, but to pay their vows to the Most High? It is conceivable that a considerable change in worship might follow if there were many men who were accustomed to say in their own hearts, Today I will go to the house of God to offer prayers and thanksgivings and celebrate the goodness of life in Him.

Having come to the house of God, what the worshiper most desires is the sense of God, an awareness of all things. He desires to pass through a door-of-leaving-behind that he may have release from manifoldness and confusion, cares and sins, perplexities, fatigues and affairs. He desires to find solution and integrity, wholeness and strength, a vision of the ineffable and the divine. The service of worship must assist this adventure, must present the reality and mediate the divine. Some presentation the usual service attempts to make. In most forms of service there are invocations, doxologies, glorias, responsive readings and other declarative elements. Through these the presence of divinity is invoked or celebrated, and by these the worshiper is assisted to the vision he has come to achieve and to the service he has come to offer. In early Christian worship, the ancient psalms were sung at the opening part of the service. A vestige of this usage is found in the Introit of the old liturgy. In a considerable number of churches today the Introit has been revived and developed into antiphonal responses between minister and choir as the opening part of the service. This usage serves at once several important functions both of form and content. As to content, it is the presentative element, the declaration of the divine life which the worshiper has come to find, and it is itself the service of God going on in the sanctuary to which the worshiper has come to offer his praise. In form, it is the preliminary announcement of the theme of the day, and the initial rhythmic movement of the liturgy, binding together minister and choristers as participants, not in a program, but in divine service.

The awareness of magnitude is followed by the sense of diminution. The vision of high and holy divinity reveals to the worshiper his faltering and failing humanity. In the presence of excellence of character or of achievement, ordinary accomplishments are put to shame. Superior finish and grace belittle slovenly work and careless temper. The first reaction to the vision of God is the spirit of humility in man. This is the low point in the experience of worship. It is the first backward swing of the great pendulum of attention. The feeling of contrast may take a variety of forms. It may be a sharp and swift stiffening to the emulation of some excellence of technique, so brief that the low point of self-condemnation involved is almost unnoticed. But the low point is there. It may be definite acknowledgment of sin and a spirit of contrition continued for hours or days. It may be a form of discouragement. I believe that at times it is a form of rebellion, an angry and baffled recognition of lesser powers and talents. In whatever form, this low point of contrast is a normal and often intense stage in the experience of worship. This element in the experience has always had recognition in services of worship. The Confiteor, the Kyrie Eleison,

the Prayer of General Confession, these are near the
beginning of the liturgies precisely because the contrition and need which they confess closely follow the
beginning of the experience. Many modern services
of worship have omitted recognition of this great
factor. That it should be restored in one form or another is beyond peradventure the counsel of good
aesthetics, good morals and good psychology alike.

Swiftly following upon belittlement comes its opposite. Forth again the great pendulum swings, out
of the world of frustration and weakness into the
tides of full and complete life. An enhancement of
vitality is the testimony of all the great mystics. It is
here especially that the sensuous influence of form in
the arts comes to assist the experience of worship.
The rhythms of form beat like waves upon the shores
of our physical being and quite literally increase all
the physical powers. If they convey, meanwhile,
great significations of being, of reality, of God, the
enlivened imagination of the worshiper receives a
great accretion of power. Not only is sin forgiven and
weakness made strong, but even mediocre talent
views a grander prospect of achievement as it recog-
nizes the divine processes with which it may coöperate
and in which the labor of its hands may be established. This great element in the experience has always found noble expression in the liturgies and at
just this point. The Gloria in Excelsis is the ancient
hymn following contrition and confession. Here the
celebration of life rises to its supreme heights in
praise and rejoicing for the floods of vitality capable

of enduring all things and hoping all things and itself performing many things.

Then again the ceaseless rhythms of alternation
move upon the worshiper in a process of recollection.
The heightened imagination begins to operate in
earthly scenes. Between the divine object and the
eyes of the beholder moves an obtruding cloud of
memory. Into the church comes the market place and
all its toils, the home and all its cares, all hopes, interests, projects and possibilities of life for review, estimate and judgment. If at the beginning of worship
it was some recent wrong or the last defeat which
bore down the worshiper to his low point, here there
is a wider range, a fuller review, possibly covering a
retrospect and forecast of many years and all their
affairs. This is the place then in the service of worship for the introduction of the major mental and
moral content of worship. In prayers, litanies and
scriptures, the total faith, history and hope of the
worshiping community is intimated. By these exercises, the personal concerns of all sorts and conditions
of men, the possibilities and potencies of persons and
societies are voiced and given fresh interpretation in
the divine light.

This fresh interpretation is itself the recurring
sense of divinity now experienced as illumination.
From the point of view now attained, nothing looks
the same. The materials are the same stubborn facts
of nature and human nature, of hardship and desire,
of duty and joy, but they are rearranged. Problems
are clarified and desires purified. Responsibilities are

accepted and wishes reordered. What seemed important sinks in the scale, the great values emerge and are freshly cherished. Now we know what is worth while, now our timid loyalties are enlarged into overmastering convictions. This is therefore the place in the service for the expression of convictions. A creed is a statement of the great worths of life as we most highly conceive them. I am myself convinced of the great value in worship of some form of *credo*, recited together by all the people. In our own service of worship we use differing statements but surround them by an ascription and gloria sung by the congregation in order to emphasize and maintain the rhythm of the experience forth and back between the One and the many.

Here the service moves rapidly to its conclusion, as does the experience. The celebration of life has voiced its happiness, attained its vitality and reviewed its component concerns up to this point of clarity respecting its affairs. Now it must proceed to decision. Even a half-jealous desire for emulation contains a powerful urgence to creativity. How much more is the impulse to high performance kindled and specified by the more pure and tested intimations developed if such worship as we have sought to describe is successful. When the mind sees what it is right and best to do and the whole man is made more capacious to do it, the urgence to dedication is all but irresistible. The service of worship should afford opportunity for this return to the practical world with a definite purpose by some exercise of self-offering. This is the acceptable sacrifice.

There yet remains a final element which many will wish to include for the completion of the cycle of worship. Surely there should be at the end of such a supreme course of experience an integrity of being that is reconciliation and peace. This may find utterance in a simple benediction only. Possibly at times some broader expression might well be given as the final note in the symphony of themes which have been brought to their concluding harmony.

The pattern of worship then which we have suggested is a composition of these seven elements—Vision, Humility, Vitality, Recollection, Illumination, Dedication, Peace. This design of form is overlaid or intertwined by an ever present alternation, as of light and shadow, which sways the attention of the worshiper between things human and divine. The pattern thus has within itself unity and movement and rhythm. If these essential formal elements are utilized to convey a well-selected content of things new and old, they will constitute a service of worship, vivid and moving.

Permit me, finally, a reminder of our initial study of celebration, that it disclosed a double character as joy and recollection. In the experience of the ordinary arts there is said to be no desire for action. This is true so far as the represented situation goes. In the theater one does not go upon the stage to take a hand in the situation. But I believe that the desire for ac-

tion is there and that it is one of the most powerful
of human impulses. In the imagination the represented situation is often obscured by the recollected
situation as the field of active expression. The impulse to creative action kindled by beauty is nowhere
more vividly expressed than by the poet Keats.

> When I behold upon the night's starr'd face
> Huge cloudy symbols of high romance
> And think that I may never live to trace
> Their shadows. . . .

The supremacy of the art of worship is this, that the
creative desires arising out of its vitality are given
direction by the light of a fullness of recollected content not supplied by anything short of religion.

CHAPTER III

Liturgical Materials

Too often the church has not seen that provision for worship is the chief thing it has to do. . . . To be creative means to introduce new values beyond those which men have heretofore recognized and to devise new forms of conduct different from those which the established social order and the prevailing arts and sciences prescribe. . . . It would seem that worship is one of the sources out of which new creations in the art of living arise. It is in worship that new paths open up; worship is the only suitable preparation for the greatest creative artistry in all the world, the art of reshaping the total vital process of living.

HENRY NELSON WIEMAN

III.

AS we approach the selection of concrete materials for the service of worship, we face a dilemma which is perhaps peculiar to our own times. The situation is perplexing, yet it may turn out to be a peculiar opportunity. It happens that at the very moment of a renewed evaluation of older liturgical uses and materials we are also pressed with the desire to express new concerns and aspirations. There has been of late a widespread increase in the use of materials taken from the traditional liturgies of the Christian church. There is at the same time the beginning of an effort to formulate for worship experiences and faiths widely divergent from anything expressed in traditional utterances. Curiously enough, the common denominator in both these movements is liturgical. Both tend to move away from the vagaries of individual and extemporaneous expression toward the use of definite forms.

If this liturgic impulse had begun some fifty or seventy-five years ago, the problem would have been a less difficult one. It would be the problem of improving the forms without much necessary change of content. This is precisely what is going on today amongst churches not yet so much interested in the more liberal thought. Branches of the Lutheran church especially are doing very fine work artistically in the field of liturgics. They are reëstimating their own source books of worship, writing some excellent new music, and have published a beautiful new book

of *Common Service*. The Methodists have repub-
lished the Anglican service as modified by John Wes-
ley. A Methodist superintendent of my acquaintance
has conducted especially prepared services of worship
both for the inspiration and instruction of the clergy
of his district. The Disciples denomination has appointed a commission which is actively promoting the
adoption of carefully prepared services of worship.
Far more extensive than these revivals is the increased use of short fixed parts in the services of many
free churches. These are largely selections from traditional liturgies. If we could be content with this
movement for the improvement of forms only, the
work of development might proceed without much
mental complication.

Meanwhile, however, there are many churches
which desire on the one hand more noble forms of
worship and on the other a large amount of fresh
content. They wish to weave into the experience of
religion as realized in worship those ideas and ideals
which are live and animating today. Even apart from
the thoughts of a scientific age and the reforms of a
philanthropic age, speaking in religious terms only,
there is a call for the expression of the newer and
later revelations of divinity. Barring that which may
be ephemeral, though it seem important now, there is
undoubtedly much in the social outlook of present-
day thinking which amply merits expression in forms
of liturgical utterance. However difficult artistically
it may be to do this, our worship will speedily fall
into remoteness and unreality if we do not attempt

to voice our own best thoughts and ideals. There are already a considerable number of free churches using non-Biblical materials for scripture lessons. A smaller number have attempted a modern content for responsive readings. Very few have as yet gone very far in experimentation with musical settings of new materials. I shall hope in a moment to give some representative selections of such works.

Whatever new advances we desire, however, cannot wisely displace the rich treasuries of devotion accumulated in the history of our faith. The chief objection to the old is intellectual. Yet this objection is often captious and short-sighted and not always so valid as the radical supposes. I have read a number of new expressions of the spiritual life which have been studiously careful to omit any mention of God. Yet they were fairly good descriptions of the conception of God held not only by many moderns but by many ancients also. Excepting on the frontier or amongst the ignorant generally religion has never defined God in such crude concepts as it is often accused of doing. The number of straw men set up in the world's argumentation would seem scarcely to exceed the number of straw gods at which the less well-educated radicals have directed their shafts. Many religious men today have no intention of giving up the use of this majestic term for circumlocutions and vagaries, when they have been bred to fill the term with a content as subtle and competent as need be. The great liturgies of the church contain many wonderful passages in no important wise objectionable to the modern thinker.

On the other hand, they contain expressions covering
a vast field of human experience. As the plays of
Shakespeare and the great frescoes of Giotto depict
all sorts and conditions of men and many varieties of
temper and outlook, so also the great liturgies. They
are like Homer and Dante in the display of the infinite variety of human nature, need and aspiration.
The devotional literature of Christendom is for the
most part based upon a wise psychology hardly sur-
passable. In addition to this, much of it is composed
in a noble style and diction far superior to the literary
competence of the average minister.

There are many values to be derived from the use
of prepared liturgical material. It is definite instead
of vague, following the logic of the theme more ex-
actly than the average extemporaneous utterance. In
structure and climax it is commonly better than individual composition. On the whole it makes for
brevity and pertinence in the devotional exercise.

As already suggested, the use of the older and
more stately material is especially valuable in those
parts of the service which represent the divine side of
the alternating rhythm of worship. The recollective
parts of the service must express the concerns and interests of today, but those portions of the liturgy
which lead the attention of the worshiper away from
the many to the One require the noblest possible
forms. Art critics today are placing a greatly enhanced valuation on what are called the primitives as
compared to the realists and naturalists in the history
of painting. They are doing this for the same reasons

that modern workers in the pictorial and plastic arts
are using more sophisticated methods of elimination
and simplicity. These moderns are seeking the same
artistic values to be found in the primitives, values of
concentration, remoteness and essential quality. It is
because attention to the artistry of presentation in religion has lagged behind the interest of cultivated
people in the fine arts, that we do not understand
these aesthetic principles. It would be unfortunate if
the church should cast out some of its greatest treasures at the moment when the world of the arts is
placing a fresh estimate of worth upon the very artistic qualities which they contain.

The artist in worship needs therefore to be familiar with the chief source books of Christian devotion,
especially with the great Eastern liturgies, the Roman missal and the English Book of Common
Prayer. There are several books of collected services
prepared for the use of free church bodies or of local
parishes, some of which are to be had in the libraries
of liturgics, and several anthologies of prayers ancient and modern. I am more ready to suggest famil-
iarity with these materials than I am to urge their use.
The most of us bred to non-liturgical customs do not
read prayers very well, even those of our own composition. Much less can we combine successfully into
one prayer extemporaneous and read portions. Oftentimes, however, an ancient or modern collect can be
read by itself at some place in a service with great
gain. I know an academic chapel service where this
usage is observed with marked effect both in dignity

and intellectual variety. A church which has passed some of the initial difficulties of transition to the more fixed forms of worship will be able to draw freely from the older materials if it desires to do so.

Curiously enough, the parts of the historic liturgies which have found most favor amongst the free churches are minor parts, the responsals or versicles. This is because our instinct toward improvement in worship has been correct in feeling after those material elements which would transform an order of worship from a program into a service, change it from a broken series, as of concert numbers, into an uninterrupted movement, as of a drama. The use of short versicles as transitional members binds the parts, effects the desired change in mood and gives the congregation more frequent participation. In a large number of free churches, for instance, just before the first hymn of praise or the anthem, these ancient responsals are said:

O Lord, open Thou our lips,
    And our mouth shall show forth thy praise,
Praise ye the Lord,
    The Lord's name be praised.

Another familiar group may precede the principal prayer.

The Lord be with you,
    And with thy spirit.
Lift up your hearts,
    We lift them up unto the Lord.

It is no mere imitation for any church to revive the

use of these materials, for in the bulk of Christendom they have never fallen into disuse. On the whole, these and some other such minor parts of the liturgy are the most universal. No other exact forms are found amongst so many divergent bodies of Christians. They thus represent the cohesion of Christianity in a remarkable degree. One might almost say that they represent the continuity of the whole culture of the Western world as nearly as any other symbols. That cohesion and the unity of that culture are precious, and there are many men who value new things, who yet have profound passion for the wholeness of the cultural life from which we have come, and a deep longing to promote the increasing unity they hope for it in the future. It is scarcely possible to overestimate the binding and connective force of a few simple words or formulas if they are actually used by bodies of people widely divergent in race, nationality and religious conviction. The Book of Common Prayer is one of the most profound of the cohesive forces in the British Empire. The Lord's Prayer is perhaps the chief common usage of Christendom. Other things being equal, there is incalculable value not only to the unity of Christianity but also to the unity of the whole of Western culture, in maintaining such concrete expressions as have been pervasive in the past and bid fair to retain general acceptability. It is true that many are not much moved by historic sentiments nor much aware of the fateful entities of what is vaguely called Western culture. But some of us think they ought to be. And we think also that those fateful possibilities have a direct connection with the simple ordinary usages of American Protestantism. Those usages may become divisive, or they may become powerful forces of unification.

We must now turn to the notice of some concrete materials typical of current usages in worship. The passages chosen are not always selected because of superior merit in literary form or thought content, but as illustrative of actual use in some way significant to liturgical development. They are presented according as they fit into the pattern of worship already discussed as it follows the order of experience through Preparation, Vision, Humility, Vitality, Recollection, Illumination, Dedication, Peace. I do not mean to suggest that all of these elements need conscious expression in every ordinary service of worship, much less in services for extraordinary situations or occasions. Yet I am familiar with services of worship which are brief and simple though they include in some form an expression of most of these elements.

PREPARATION

The most common usage of a preparatory character is a Call to Worship comprised of one or more scripture verses. I do not quote any such because every minister can find them in the Bible, while excellent collections are published in most of the major hymn books. A little careful work at this point will discover the possibility of using phrases of scripture which are at once a Call to Worship and an indication

of the theme of the day. In this way the material becomes presentative as well as preparatory.

In many services the principal preparatory suggestion is set forth in an exhortation, such as the following:

God, in whom we live and move and have our being,
never leaves us day or night. But the very nearness and
custom of his presence hide him from our infirm and sinful
hearts, temptations gain a shameful power, and the good
that is in us droops and fades. To clear such blindness away
and recover the pure wisdom of a Christian mind, we are
called to this day of remembrance and this house of prayer.
Entering here, therefore, we cross the threshold of eternal
things and commune with the Father who seeth in secret.
Let us shake off the dust of transitory care, and every dis-
guise that can come between us and God; and remembering
whose disciples we strive to be, come to the simplicity,
though it should be also to the sorrows, of the Christ.[1]

Similar in preparatory intention, but of different content is an invitation to worship written by Israel
Zangwill:

Come into the circle of Love and Justice,
Come into the Brotherhood of Pity,
Of Holiness and Health!
Come, and ye shall know Peace and Joy.
Let what ye desire of the Universe penetrate you,
Let Loving Kindness and Mercy pass through you,
And Truth be the Law of your mouth.
For so ye are channels of the divine sea,
Which may not flood the earth, but only steal in
Through rifts in your souls.[2]

[1] *Hymn and Tune Book.*   [2] Stanton Coit, *Social Worship.*

A brief admonition of direct and forceful suggestiveness is one of Mr. Stanton Coit's:

Let none who are here present remain mere critics or spectators. Let us all be communicants in the moral life of this meeting, entering into its devotion with a spirit of comradeship, with a becoming sense of our several needs, and with reverence for the ideal of human character.

From a service order of the West Side Unitarian Church of New York City are taken these words of aspiration, which properly fall under the element of spiritual preparation:

From our widely scattered and distant homes we come to this our house of fellowship and aspiration. Bound by a common purpose and a common problem we unite in mutual aid. Free from every untruth, however delightful, we would search and find life's meaning and its glory. We come to furbish our ideals, to redevote ourselves to the best we know, to recall our covenants with ourselves and others, and to set ourselves anew to the task of living. May the comradeship of kindred souls assist us, the knowledge that others share our hopes, our difficulties, and our failures, encourage us. This is our great covenant, to dwell together in peace, to seek the truth in love, and to help one another.

One or two faults of construction or diction in this paragraph are obvious. There was probably no intention to make the claim of being free from every untruth but rather of a desire to be so free. The word *furbish* is not an entirely happy metaphor. But let not these slight ineptitudes blind appreciation of the vigor, genuineness and breadth of this expression. It must be remembered that this is a "mine run" paragraph, one of many such prepared freshly each week by a busy minister. This is what makes it valuable. If far larger numbers of ministers took as much pains with their service of worship every week as this indicates, we should soon have an overflowing abundance of rich and vital liturgical material from which to make selection for every requirement.

Still under the category of Preparation is the usual Invocation. For the most part amongst the free churches this preparatory prayer is an extemporaneous utterance. I quote some which have been published as indicative of excellent material for this point in the service:

O God, the King eternal, who dividest the day from the darkness and turnest the shadow of death into the morning, drive far from us all wrong desires, incline our hearts to keep thy law, and guide our feet into the way of peace; that, having done thy will with cheerfulness while it was day, we may, when the night cometh, rejoice to give thee thanks. Amen.

O Lord our God, who hast bidden the light to shine out of darkness and who hast again wakened us to praise thy goodness and ask for thy grace; accept now, in thy endless mercy, the sacrifice of our worship and thanksgiving, and grant unto us all such gifts as may be wholesome for us. Make us to be children of the light and of the day, and heirs of thine unfailing inheritance; so that we, being made whole in soul and body, and steadfast in faith may ever praise thy wonderful and holy name. Amen.[1]

[1] *Hymn and Tune Book.*

For Christmas.

O loving Father, who has brought us again to the glad season when we commemorate the birth of thy Son, Jesus of Nazareth, grant that his spirit may be born anew in our hearts this day and that we may joyfully welcome him to reign over us. Open our ears that we may hear again the angelic chorus of old; open our lips that we too may sing with uplifted hearts, Glory to God in the highest, and on earth peace, good will toward men.　　　　Amen.[1]

For Easter.

O Lord and Giver of life, who dost renew the face of the earth with singing and joyful loveliness, renew in our hearts an unconquered faith in the beauty of holiness. Even as the spirit of Christ arose triumphant over the bitter pain of the cross and the darkness of the tomb, enable us to look beyond the things of earth which pass away and to find our joy and peace in thine infinite and eternal life. Give us such trust and confidence in thy love that we may know ourselves to be ever in thine hand, and uplift our souls to worship thee in spirit and in truth, at one in heart and voice with the great company of those who have walked in thy light and who stand in joy before thee.　　　　Amen.[1]

For Children's Sunday.

O God, our Father, from thy hand has come every blessing which gives us joy and comfort. Thou dost speak to us through the love of our mothers, through the guiding care of our fathers. Help us to worship thee as the all-holy love who dost inspire every pure affection; as the infinite wisdom who art the revealer of all truth; as the almighty power who dost uphold us in life. As we grow day by day in stature help us to grow in grace, that we may gladly serve thee and our fellow-men in righteousness and love.

Amen.[1]

[1] Henry Wilder Foote.

As already suggested, some ministers find it very difficult to take any account liturgically of this matter of preparation for worship. One other method is frequently used, the Processional Hymn. Although the content of ideas in the hymn may not always be of a preparatory character, the psychological effect of its use is of that sort. It gathers attention, begins to merge the individual worshipers into a congregation, and often initiates the rhythmic motion of the service.

PRESENTATION

Those services which begin with a considerable amount of preparatory material will hardly find place for much declarative expression at the opening of the service. If, on the other hand, material which takes account of the subjective attitude of the worshiper is slight or omitted altogether, there is opportunity for a strong presentative element. The most interesting form of presentation now being more and more used is the Introit. The chief problem of the usage is the music. The statements by the minister may be freshly prepared for every service. The antiphons sung by the choir must of course be fitted to music. There is only a meager amount of music suitable for this usage. Those genuinely interested to experiment will find materials. As the one single best publication available, I suggest a book published by the United Lutheran Publication House, Philadelphia, *Introits and Graduals* by Matthews. This is simply an agreeable musical setting of the traditional

Introits in English. Many of them are not usable in modern churches for theological reasons, and some for ethical reasons. Oftentimes an antiphon for one day may be combined with a portion of the Introit or a Gradual from another day in order to make up such responsive numbers as I am suggesting. In actual practice this is a simple thing to do. The Introits given below are not prepared especially for publication but are presented as having been actually used in services of worship, some prepared with more care than others.

The words of the first selection were chosen to open a service in which the sermon subject was Religious Comprehension. The music used was that of Matthews, the first response being taken from the ancient Introit for Transfiguration and the second being the Gradual for the fourth Sunday in Lent.

MINISTER:
Thus saith the Lord—
I am the Lord and there is none else; there is no God beside me:
I girded thee though thou has not known me.
I form the light and create darkness:
I make peace and create evil:
   I the Lord do all these things.
And there is no God beside me: a just God and a Savior.
Look unto me and be ye saved, all the ends of the earth:
For I am God and there is none else.

CHOIR:
The lightnings lightened the world;
   The earth trembled and shook.

How amiable are thy tabernacles,
   O Lord, Lord of hosts:
My soul longeth, yea even fainteth for thy courts,
   The courts of the Lord.

MINISTER:

Sing unto the Lord, and give thanks at the remembrance of
      his holiness.
Some trust in chariots and some in horses:
But we will remember the name of the Lord our God.
Whoso offereth praise glorifieth me:
And to him that ordereth his conversation aright will I show
      the salvation of God.

CHOIR:

I was glad when they said unto me:
   Let us go into the house of the Lord.
Peace be within thy walls:
   And prosperity within thy palaces.
They that trust in the Lord shall be as Mount Zion:
   Which cannot be removed, but abideth forever.

The following Introit introduced a service devoted
to the Social Gospel. The three choir responses are
generic wordings suitable to a variety of themes of
the active character, set to music privately printed:

MINISTER:

I will praise thee, O Lord, with my whole heart:
I will show forth all thy marvelous works.
I will sing praise unto thy name, O thou Most High.
   The Lord shall endure forever:
He has prepared his throne for judgment.
And he shall judge the world in righteousness,
The Lord will be a refuge for the oppressed.

CHOIR:

Bless the Lord, all his works,
In all places of his dominion:
Bless the Lord, O my soul.

MINISTER:

Therefore all things whatsoever ye would that men should
           do to you,
Do ye even so to them: for this is the law and the prophets.

CHOIR:

Bless the Lord, all ye his hosts:
Ye ministers of his that do his pleasure.
Bless the Lord, O my soul.

MINISTER:

Light is sown for the righteous, and gladness for the up-
           right in heart.
The righteous shall be in everlasting remembrance and the
           memory of the just shall be blessed.
The faithful in love shall abide in him.
Their reward is with the Lord,
And the care of them is with the Most High.

CHOIR:

And his servants shall serve him:
And they shall see his face.
Bless the Lord, all his hosts.
Bless the Lord, bless the Lord, O my soul.

Amongst materials from outside the Bible, suitable
for occasional use for Introits, the beautiful Canticle
of Saint Francis of Assisi is one of the most acceptable. Music by Helen Goodrich for the portion indicated has been published.

MINISTER:

O most high, almighty, good Lord God, to thee belong praise, glory, honor, and all blessing.

Praised be my Lord God with all his creatures, and especially our brother the sun, who brings us the day and who brings us the light; fair is he and shines with a very great splendor: O Lord, he signifies to us thee.

Praised be my Lord for our sister the moon, and for the stars, the which he has set clear and lovely in heaven.

Praised be my Lord for our brother the wind, and for air and cloud, calms and all weather by the which thou upholdest life in all creatures.

Praised be my Lord for our sister water, who is very serviceable unto us and humble and precious and clean.

Praised be my Lord for our brother fire, through which thou givest us light in the darkness; and he is bright and pleasant and very mighty and strong.

CHOIR:

Praised be my Lord for our mother the earth, the which doth sustain us and keep us, and bringeth forth divers fruits and flowers of many colors, and grass.

MINISTER:

Praised be my Lord for all those who pardon one another for his love's sake, and who endure weakness and tribulation; blessed are they who peaceably shall endure, for thou, O most Highest, shalt give them a crown.

Praised be my Lord for our sister, the death of the body, from which no man escapeth. Woe to him who dieth in mortal sin. Blessed are they who are found walking by thy most holy will, for the second death shall have no power to do them harm.

Praise ye and bless the Lord, and give thanks unto him and serve him with great humility.

CHOIR:

Praised be my Lord for our mother the earth, the which doth sustain us and keep us, and bringeth forth divers fruits and flowers of many colors, and grass.

Sometimes it is effective to use the same general theme through more than one service. For the season of Advent, music has been written by Mr. Leo Sowerby to words of responses suggestive of expectancy. The minister's parts may be varied while the antiphons of the choir sustain the Advent theme.

MINISTER:

Out of Zion the perfection of beauty, God hath shined.
    Our God shall come and shall not keep silence.
Behold thy salvation cometh,
The Lord shall cause his glorious voice to be heard;
    And ye shall have gladness of heart.

CHOIR:

Lift up your heads, O ye gates;
And be ye lift up, ye everlasting doors;
And the king of glory shall come in.
    The Lord of hosts.

MINISTER:

Open ye the gates that the righteous nation which keepeth
        truth may enter in.
Seek ye the Lord while he may be found.
Call ye upon him while he is near.
Hope thou in God—for I shall yet praise him for the help
        of his countenance.

CHOIR:

Prepare your hearts unto the Lord.
Prepare your hearts unto the Lord, unto the Lord.

MINISTER:

Behold the Lord will come with strong hand and his arm
  shall rule for him:
Behold his reward is with him and his work before him.
He shall feed his flock like a shepherd:
He shall gather the lambs in his arms and carry them in his
  bosom:
And shall gently lead them that are with young.
They shall not hurt nor destroy in all my holy mountain,
For the earth shall be full of knowledge of the Lord, as the
  waters cover the sea.

CHOIR:

Prepare, Prepare the way of the Lord.
Make straight in the desert
  An highway for our God.

It is to be hoped that there may be more and better
music available for antiphonal responses in the early
future. This can hardly come, however, as a theoreti-
cal development only. It must arise out of experiment and actual use. The many advantages in dignity,
worshipful quality and impressiveness to be derived
from the use of a choral Introit should prompt many
experiments in new musical composition. Some com-
posers interested in church music are producing large
and brilliant works for extraordinary occasions. Few
are dealing in a large way with the problem of the
more simple musical works necessary for successful
conduct of ordinary worship in a liturgical manner.
Those who might care to use extra-Biblical materials
for antiphonal responses will find a variety of poems
with music in Stanton Coit's *Social Worship*. The

musical settings of these are derived largely from the ancient Gregorian modes. In any case, the development of better materials for the opening part of the service of worship is one of the most interesting opportunities for constructive work in liturgics.

HUMILITY

Following next after a vivid experience or vision of reality comes the sense of belittlement or humility. All the old liturgies contain vigorous expressions of penitence. Many free church services have revived in some form a prayer of confession. I know of no liturgical expression of the rebellious reaction which sometimes the experience of a great magnitude produces. In its cruder forms, this would not be suitable for devotional expression. Possibly sometime, however, some minister will compose a good prayer expressive of the spiritual need of those whose sense of belittlement is not a sense of shame, but of disappointment or defeat due to lesser talents. The most common penitential prayers revived for use amongst the free churches are the General Confession from the English Prayer Book and some adaptation of the Fifty-first Psalm. These are both grand compositions with a minimum of intellectual difficulty. I quote two or three other prayers amongst the best that I have noted from current materials.

Prayer of Confession.

Almighty Lord of heaven and earth, Before thee and one another we do confess our sins in thought, and word, and deed. We do earnestly repent all our misdoings, And of any whom we may have wronged we seek forgiveness. With thy help we would overcome our faults, And in the spirit of Jesus Christ would faithfully serve thee and our fellow-men, All the days of our life.   Amen.

Prayer of Confession.

O Thou unseen source of peace and holiness, may we come into Thy secret place and be filled with Thy pure and solemn light.

As we come to Thee, how can we but remember where we have been drawn aside from the straight and narrow way, where we have not walked lovingly with each other and humbly with Thee, where we have feared what is not terrible and wished for what is not holy. In our weakness be Thou the quickening power of life. Arise within our hearts as healing, strength and joy.

Day by day we grow in faith, in charity, in the purity by which we may see Thee, and the larger life of love to which Thou callest us.   Amen.

Prayer of Confession.

Have compassion, O God, upon thy servants; seeing that our hearts are grieved for having offended against thee, and our consciences condemn us, and we have no refuge save only in thy mercy, which thou hast revealed through Jesus Christ, our Lord.   Amen.

Prayer of Confession.

Source of all good! Day by day are thy blessings renewed to us; and again we come with thankful hearts to seek the sense of thy presence. O that we could be reborn like the morning. For even as we seek to commune with thee shadows from our past dim the joy of our aspiration. We remember our thoughtless lives, our impatient tempers, our selfish aims; and yet we know that thou hast neither made us blind like the creatures that have no sin, nor left us

without holy guidance—thy still, small voice speaking in
our inmost conscience, and thine open word, having dwelt
among us full of grace and truth, appealing to us to choose
the better part.   Amen.

VITALITY

The rhythm of alternation, moving from weakness to strength, finds expression in the great hymns
of praise. This is the place in the service most commonly given to the anthem. Many churches, however, are finding the anthem an increasing problem.
Not only are the words of many anthems unsuitable
for modern religion, but much of the musical literature is secular in quality. Perhaps paradoxically,
many churches are looking for anthems which have a
more progressive outlook in content combined with
more religious spirit in the musical form. Probably
the best brief collection of material is the *Concord
Anthem Book* edited by Davison and Foote. Another
difficulty about the anthem is that of merging it into
the stream of the service. It often gives the impression of a concert number rather than an integral portion of a moving and unified liturgy. It is for this
reason that many churches use at this point simply a
hymn of praise sung by the congregation. I am per-
sonally sometimes accused of desiring to elaborate
worship, and therefore wish to report that in our own
church we have discarded the anthem for the more
simple congregational hymn.

Another resource for the expression of praise is the
Responsive Reading. The Psalms together with a
few other Biblical passages and church Canticles con-

tinue to be the chief source materials for congregational reading. A few churches have made experiments in the responsive reading of modern compositions. It is easier to criticize these attempts to put a fresh content into this ancient exercise than it is to produce others as good. The examples quoted are taken from the actual service orders as used in the Unitarian churches of Toledo and Los Angeles.

The spirit of Man shall triumph and reign o'er all the earth.

The earth was made for Man, he is heir to all that therein is.

He is the end of creation, the purpose of the ages since the dawn of time.

He is the fulfillment of all prophecy and in himself the goal of every great hope born in high desire.

Who art Thou, O Spirit of Man?

Thou art the Child of the Infinite, in thy nostrils is the breath of God.

Thou didst come at Love's behest, yea! to fulfill the Love of the Eternal didst Thou come.

Yet Man's beginnings were in lowliness, in nature akin to that of the brute.

His body and appetite bore the marks of the beast, yet in his soul was the unquenchable Spark of Divine Fire.

His ascending hath been with pain, with struggle and conflict hath he marched toward the Ideal.

At times he hath turned his face away from the Promise of Destiny.

He hath given reins to the lust of the brute; he hath appeared at times as the Child of Hate.

He hath forgotten his Divine Origin, he hath forsaken the dream of Eternal Love.

Then hath he lifted his hands against his fellows and war and bloodshed have dwelt upon the earth.

In moments of blind passion he hath destroyed the work of his own hands, the fruit of the centuries hath he cast to the winds.

He hath marred the Divine Image, deaf to the call of the Promise of God.

Upon the altars of Self hath he sacrificed Brotherhood, and ruled by avarice and greed he hath slain Justice and Right.

Thus have wickedness and sin dwelt in his midst, and his soul hath been chained in the bondage of low desires.

Yet all this could not destroy the unquenchable Spark of Divine Fire.

For it belongs to the Eternal and that which is Eternal cannot die.

Therefore, great though Thy shortcomings, manifold though Thy failure, wicked though Thy crimes;

I will not despair, O spirit of Man!

Though Thou destroyest fairest hopes yet shall they live again.

Though Thou returnest to the level of the beast Thou shalt arise to the heights of Thy Divine Humanity.

For the spirit of Man breathes the untiring purpose of the Living God and to the fulfillment of that purpose the whole creation moves.

The author of this reading has recognized that its purposes are not merely intellectual but also artistic. He has sought to achieve the desired remoteness or distance by retaining something of the archaic style of diction. Moreover, he has succeeded in a marked degree in achieving a rhythmic movement which gives a poetic spirit to the composition and makes an immediate appeal to the senses. All these things are extremely difficult and merit the warm approval of those seriously interested in a vital development for new reality and power in worship. The next selection abandons the archaic style, but it has vigor, freshness and simplicity and achieves a certain measure of rhythm despite its prosaic form.

There is a law in man's being, sacred, inviolable, revealed in his sense of what he ought to be and do.

This higher law—the law above all laws—rests not on our consent. It is here commanding us whether we consent or not.

It is not imposed from without but given in the very nature of man.

Man is made for the good; starting imperfect he is called to be perfect.

We are here to lift ourselves to the measure of perfect goodness.

Life is not for living merely, but for a perfect life that each may live here as the citizen of an ideal kingdom.

The higher law is that which commands us to seek the universal good.

Not food nor raiment nor shelter; not comfort nor ease; not science nor art are the ends of existence, but the "kingdom of God."

Seek ye first the kingdom of God and his righteousness.

When man obeys the inner command he feels the freshness of an eternal day in his heart.

When a man says, "I ought"; when love warms him; when he chooses, warned from on high, the good and great deed,

Then deep melodies wander through his soul from Supreme Wisdom.

He who does a good deed is instantly ennobled.

If a man is at heart just, then in so far is he God; the safety of God, the immortality of God, the majesty of God do enter into that man with justice.

The stars in heaven are not so grand as a man living in obedience to the higher law, or dying when it is better not to live.

We belong to peace; we belong to love; we belong to all that is covered by the sacred name of Good.

O let us count for good, for purity, for unselfishness, for all that makes human life strong and stable on the earth.

Another selection attains a considerable reminiscence of ancient form by the use of a single archaic word only. And by repetitive phrases it attains and increases momentum to an especially vigorous climax.

Through the long centuries of human history there has been building a Beloved Community in which all souls that love, all souls that aspire, are bound together in one life.

Precious unto us are the names of the heroes and leaders of the race who have toiled mightily in the service of the Beloved Community.

Precious unto us are the men of the spirit of Jesus, who, in every age and every clime, have endured all things that they might bear testimony to that truth which is powerful unto the salvation of the world.

Precious unto us is the memory of the unnumbered millions who humble and nameless the straight hard pathway have trod.

Precious unto us the memory of earth's lowly who have

added, each in his measure, to the ever growing treasures of the common life of man.

All these have not lived in vain.

They have put on immortality in the life of the Beloved Community.

All these are not dead.

They have joined the Choir Invisible whose music is the gladness of the world.

Still does the spirit of Jesus speed on its conquering way.

Still do the Prophets and Martyrs inspire men to heroism and self-sacrifice in the service of life.

Still do our own beloved dead live again in minds made better by their presence.

We too are members of the Beloved Community. A thousand unseen ties bind us in one living body apart from which there is no life.

We are joined in one communion of love and aspiration with all mankind, living and dead.

We too have our gifts to bring to the altar of Humanity, —gifts of love, of wisdom, of consecration.

We too would make our contribution to the unborn future, and find immortality in the radiant life of the Beloved Community.

We are strong with the strength of all mankind; the courage of Humanity's burden bearers of all the years descends upon us.

We are thine, O Beloved Community! Take us, use us! Let our whole lives be an offering laid on thy living altar.

I know of no published volumes of modern responsive readings excepting *Readings from Great Authors*, arranged by John Haynes Holmes and others. Some of the selections are usable, while others fail of the rhythmic and poetic quality necessary to successful responsive reading. The problems of the responsive reading have led many to abandon it altogether and to transfer the desirable congregational participation to other parts of the service, including some form of litany.

RECOLLECTION

After the initial acts of worship, of approach, confession and praise and the exercises which have assisted their performance with genuine and moving feeling, the service is ready for a more definite mental and moral content. This is afforded by scripture readings and prayers. Although only a few churches have begun the custom of extra-Biblical scripture readings, there is already an abundance of excellent material for the purpose. The large volume I of *Social Worship* by Stanton Coit is a mine of valuable selections. More recently published is an excellent but much smaller compilation, *Great Companions*, arranged by Robert French Leavens. Two useful collections of poetic material are *The World's Great Religious Poetry*, edited by Caroline Miles Hill, and *Modern Religious Verse and Prose*, compiled by Fred Merrifield. Undoubtedly the development of an expanded lectionary will receive increasing attention in the early future. Nothing in the way of authoritative compilations may be expected soon, but there is need for further experiment and publication of religious readings for church services. I should not be surprised to see in the chancel of some church, beside the lectern, a suitable bookrack containing various translations of the Biblical scriptures and certain volumes of extra-Biblical scriptures ready at hand for use in the service.

For the most of the free churches, fixed and read prayers are not generally acceptable. My own preference is for the maintenance of the custom of free and spontaneous prayer, despite the many objections to it and the low level of achievement in it. It tends to become monotonous and meager in content as compared with the wealth and variety of liturgical prayer. It tends to length and reiteration. It tends to shocking improprieties of material, structure and diction. At a recent community service which I attended, a prayer by a preacher of national reputation began with the quotation of a whole quatrain of rhymed verse. If such a man could make so glaring a mistake, it is ample evidence of a general lack of the best critical canons in this matter. The objection in this particular instance is not merely literary but imaginative and spiritual. No one who had himself made the initial preparation of spirit for the solemn act of prayer could begin the utterance with a series of rhymes. I believe, therefore, that genuine, inner readiness of spirit to pray somehow improves the very style of speech. This is not to say that the spirit of prayer alone is sufficient to assure good diction without attention to the technique of style. The advantage of prepared prayers is that the excellence of style, which means the suitability of the medium to the theme, is of marked assistance to the spirit.

I do not quote examples of the many available col-
lects. Every minister should possess copies of certain
modern collections of brief prayers as well as the
older prayer books. The older prayers are for the
most part superior not only in style but in the variety
of the spiritual need and aspiration voiced. It is difficult to find good written prayers which give expression to the urgencies of present-day ethics. The two
prayers following are presented as expressive of the
outlooks of modern morals, though both have stylis-
tic faults. They are taken from *Modern Prayers*,
edited by Samuel McComb, D.D.

Prayer For International Good Will—S. T. Gulick.

O Thou, who hast made of one blood all nations of men,
help us to see the largeness and wisdom of Thy ways. Thou
dost love all men and dost yearn to bring them into the fulness of Thine own rich life. While we glory in the Christ
whom Thou hast given us, preserve us, Heavenly Father,
from spiritual arrogance and race pride. Open our eyes to
the goodness and truth Thou hast revealed to others. Make
us more like Christ who rejoiced in the faith of the Roman
centurion and praised the noble deeds of the good Samari-
tan. Hasten the day when race pride and prejudice shall
vanish from the earth and universal goodwill prevail. Forgive, O Lord, our narrowness, our selfishness, our pride and
lead us into the fulness of Thine own infinite life. Make
us in truth Thy children: through Christ our Lord.

Amen.

A Merchant's Prayer—L. E. D. Hewins.

Lord Jesus, give us wisdom to understand and a will to
obey Thy teaching concerning riches and poverty, buying

and selling, and the conduct of business between man and man. Never let us forget the order of industry is based on those spiritual principles Thou hast taught the world. Grant to the merchant, the producer, the employee, the consumer to know the laws of fair compensation and profit, and help us to realize that in all our business dealings we are called to serve our fellows, to bless them, not to injure them. Grant that we may never desire to take something for nothing, and when we give, may it be with thoughtfulness and with due regard to the interests of the giver and the taker, so that those whom we serve may prosper in things spiritual and in things material. For Thy Name's sake, Amen.

One of the ancient usages of form which is finding more and more favor is the Responsive Prayer or Litany. It has several advantages. It affords a direct and natural method of congregational participation in public devotions. It gives the sense of finish and adequate preparation to the service. It yields the benefits of fixed form without some of the dangers of formalism when the minister only reads fixed prayers. It usually provides a wealth of content expressed in the most brief way. The first example selected is for general devotional use in an ordinary service of worship. In this instance, the response of the people is sung.

Litany.
MINISTER:
 Almighty and eternal God, source of the light that never sets and of the love that never fails, life of our life, father of our spirits, draw us to Thyself in trust and love.
 By all the meaning and the wonder of Thy order which

rules over all; by the beauty which shines through all; by the ever wider knowledge and deeper life which blesses all:

PEOPLE:

Teach us and lead us ever nearer to Thee.

MINISTER:

By the revelation of Thyself in the lives of all wise, great and good men; by the strength and grace which shine for us in the face of Jesus Christ; by every living word of truth and by every good example; by the fellowship, joy and praise of Thy holy church:

PEOPLE:

Teach us and lead us ever nearer to Thee.

MINISTER:

By the kindness and love which have been about us from the beginning of our days even until now; by the relations of home; by the love of little children; by the faithful loyalty of friends; by the very trials and bereavements which chasten and deepen our life; by all the blessed memories of our dead:

PEOPLE:

Teach us and lead us ever nearer to Thee.

MINISTER:

By the conflict of our souls with temptation; by our mistakes and failures; by our shame and repentance; by every holy aspiration, striving, and victory:

PEOPLE:

Teach us and lead us ever nearer to Thee.

MINISTER:

By all our experience; in health and in sickness; in joy and sorrow; in every circumstance and in every place, O God, our Father:

PEOPLE:

Teach us and lead us ever nearer to Thee.   Amen.

Another composition of a generic spiritual content is adapted from H. Youlden as published in *Social Worship*.

Litany of Thanksgiving.

MINISTER:

Let us join in the tumult of praise ceaselessly resounding throughout creation. With stars that sing and skies that smile, with the exuberance and beauty of the life of nature, with the voices and hearts of the children of men: with saints and seers and prophets, with those whose craftsmanship is their song, with all who find in human service their joy made full.

CONGREGATION:

We lift up our hearts in gratitude and praise.

MINISTER:

In life, its adventures, risks and prizes, in the strength of the soul that overcomes all dangers,

CONGREGATION:

We rejoice with thanksgiving.

MINISTER:

In tasks that are hard, in work well done, in the skill of our hands, in experience, judgment, decision,

CONGREGATION:

We rejoice with thanksgiving.

MINISTER:

In knowledge, in joining fact to fact, in seeing truth in its beauty,

CONGREGATION:

We rejoice with thanksgiving.

MINISTER:

In health, in sickness that has passed away, in sorrows that have not visited us, in temptation that did not tarry at our door, in fears that turned to triumph,

CONGREGATION:

We rejoice with thanksgiving.

MINISTER:

In the faces of those we love, in eyes that look kindly upon us even when we fail, in those with whom we are at rest,

CONGREGATION:

We rejoice with thanksgiving.

MINISTER:

In those who though dead, yet speak, the known and the unknown, the great and the lowly, by whose lives we are enabled to live,

CONGREGATION:

We rejoice with thanksgiving.

MINISTER:

In the occasions when we humbled ourselves and chose the way of meekness, in the things we did which were wiser than we knew, in the unexpected strength that came to us in the hour of weakness and despair,

CONGREGATION:

We rejoice with thanksgiving.

MINISTER:

In time that heals every wound, makes every rough place plain and every crooked thing straight,

CONGREGATION:

We rejoice with thanksgiving.

MINISTER:

In the Life that rules the world, at whose feet we do our work and in whose arms we fall asleep,

CONGREGATION:

We rejoice and will rejoice: we give thanks and will give thanks. Let the work of our hands declare the gladness of our hearts and kindly deeds speak forth the gratitude within.

From a book of *Acts of Devotion* comes a prayer with something more of the modern ethical content.

Brief Litany.

For ministers and all who guide the thoughts of the people by their writings; for all artists, poets, dramatists, musicians and journalists; that inspired by pure ideals, our common life may be crowned with beauty and vision;

We beseech Thee to hear us, good Lord.

For all who champion the cause of the poor, and all who seek to set free those whose toil can bring no joy, that they may be saved from bitterness and disappointment, and in all things seek first the kingdom of God;

We beseech Thee to hear us, good Lord.

For all who heal the body, guard the health of the people and tend the sick; that they may follow in the footsteps of Christ, the great Physician both of the body and soul;

We beseech Thee to hear us, good Lord.

For all on whose labor we depend for the necessaries of life, and for those who carry on the commerce of the world; that they may seek no private gain which would hinder the good of all;

We beseech Thee to hear us, good Lord.

In a Christmas Service at Beloit College, the following vigorous and beautiful Responsive Prayer was used.

Christmas Litany.

MINISTER:

Glory to God in the highest.

CONGREGATION:

And on earth peace among men in whom he is well pleased.

MINISTER:

Let us pray:

O God, Thou art our salvation, we will trust and not be afraid. Thou art our strength and song.

CONGREGATION:

Therefore with joy shall we draw water out of the wells of salvation.

MINISTER:

We thank Thee for the birth of Jesus, that Thy spirit was upon him, that he was anointed to preach good tidings to the poor, to proclaim release to the captive, the recovering of sight to the blind, to set at liberty them that are bruised.

CONGREGATION:

Help us to make our present world the acceptable year of the Lord.

MINISTER:

O God, enable us, as we worship Thee, to kindle with the joy of simple shepherds long ago, at the thought of all that came to the world in the birth of the child Jesus.

CONGREGATION:

Cast out our sin and enter in; be born in us today.

MINISTER:

Help us, O God, in the light of the shining star to realize the wastes and desolations of the world, to feel the weight of the world's sorrow and need, to be made aware of the power of evil, to see what spiritual loss is caused by man's hatreds and sins.

CONGREGATION:

Help us with Jesus' spirit to build the old wastes and to raise up the former generations.

MINISTER:

Forgive us, O God, for our weariness of heart after great conflict and exertion. Suffer us not to become creatures and nations of selfishness, of narrow foolish pride, marred with hardness of heart and weakened by fear and suspicion.

CONGREGATION:

Grant unto us that we being delivered out of the hand of our enemies may serve Thee without fear.

MINISTER:

Help us to build America in love rather than in provincial selfishness; help us here to keep America a land of hope for all mankind; help us to find in our patriotism the cross of humanity's desires.

CONGREGATION:

May the dayspring from on high visit us, to shine upon us when in darkness we lose our faith in Thee.

These examples of litanies are sufficient to indicate the practicability of the form. Probably few churches would care to use such a prayer in every service. If for any reason it is desirable to omit a Responsive Reading from the Psalms or other writings, then the litany form of prayer may very well supply the valuable congregational share in the service. It is a form especially adapted to the great festal services of the church year or other extraordinary occasions. It is a form, moreover, in which original composition is more likely to be successful than in some other parts of the liturgy.

ILLUMINATION

Because of the prevailing distaste, not to say contempt, for creeds, little progress has been made by way of modern statements of faith. Those who have tried to make such statements have at once discovered that it is extremely difficult to produce anything of sufficiently dignified and rhythmic style for congregational recital. The examples quoted are not presented as satisfactory but as actual usages.

Confession of Faith.

We believe in God, the Father of our spirits, the life of all that is: infinite in power, wisdom, and goodness, and working everywhere for righteousness and peace and love.

We believe in the ideal of human life which reveals itself in Jesus as love to God and love to man.

We believe that we should be ever growing in knowledge and ever aiming at a higher standard of character.

We believe in the growth of the kingdom of God on earth, and that our loyalty to truth, to righteousness, and to our fellow men, is the measure of our desire for its coming.

We believe that the living and the dead are in the hands of God; that underneath both are His everlasting arms.

A Scriptural Confession of Faith.

God is a spirit, and they that worship him must worship him in spirit and in truth. God is light and in him is no darkness at all, neither shadow that is cast by turning. God is love and every one that loveth is begotten of God and knoweth God. Love never faileth, and there is no fear in love, but perfect love casteth out fear. So then we are debtors not to the flesh to live after the flesh, but we received the spirit of adoption whereby we cry Abba, Father. Being therefore always of good courage and knowing that whilst we are at home in the body we are absent from the Lord, for we walk by faith not by sight, we make it our aim, whether at home or absent, to be well pleasing unto him. For we know that, to them that love God, all things work together for good.

Confession of Faith.

We believe that God is Spirit, and they that worship Him must worship Him in spirit and in truth.

We believe that God is Light, and if we walk in the light, as He is in the light, we have fellowship one with another.

We believe that God is Love, and every one that loveth is born of God and knoweth Him.

We believe that Jesus is the Son of God and that God hath given us eternal life, and this life is in His Son.

We believe that we are children of God, and that He hath given us of His spirit.

We believe that if we confess our sins, He is faithful and just to forgive us our sins.

We believe the world passeth away, and the lust thereof; but that he that doeth the will of God abideth forever.

Amen.

In a few services I have found some extensive expressions of faith, sometimes arranged for Responsive Reading. The following sentences are excerpts from formulations of Tolstoi and R. Roberts.

I believe in God, who is for me spirit, love, the principle of all things.

I believe that God is in me, as I am in him.

I believe that the reason for life is for each of us simply to grow in love.

I believe that this growth in love will contribute more than any other force to establish the Kingdom of God on earth—

To replace a social life in which division, falsehood and violence are all-powerful with a new order in which humanity, truth and brotherhood will reign.

I believe that the will of God has never been more clearly, more freely expressed than in the teaching of the man Jesus.

I believe that this teaching will give welfare to all humanity, save men from destruction, and give this world the greatest happiness.

Jesus' teaching is goodness and truth. Its essence is the unity of mankind, the love of men for one another.

I believe that the fulfillment of the teaching of Jesus is possible.

I believe in the transcendental meaning and hope of Life.

I believe that the real values of life are the good, the true and the beautiful.

I believe in the practicability of the Kingdom of God, and in freedom to choose it and to work for it.

I believe in the sacramental quality of my day's work and that I may see and serve God in it.

I believe in a grace that can overcome my selfishness and pride, and that will enable me to overcome temptation, and upon which I need never call in vain.

I believe in love as the final law of life.

Despite the many difficulties which are obvious, there is great value in a common recital of conviction. Here is a genuine opportunity for invention and development. It is perhaps an extremely presumptuous thing to attempt comprehensive statements. The times are not favorable to the production of creedal formularies comparable to the ancient expressions. But the times are favorable for the statement of definite items of conviction such as are actually representative of the local church at worship. Our worship could be much enriched if on special occasions the service contained brief expressions of those things actually cherished and valued amongst us. Such statements might be limited to particular regions of importance or value, such as nature, industry, human association or others when the service themes are devoted to these regions. Such a simple usage might do something to mitigate the perhaps too prevalent objection to creedal formularies, and prepare the ground for more ambitious and comprehensive efforts.

DEDICATION

Protestant services in general have failed to develop any vigorous and moving exercise of consecration. The omission of this aspect of worship involved in the abandonment of the sacramental system is one of the most profound losses of the free churches. The exercise of dedication is essentially sacramental. It is difficult in the brief ordinary service of worship to include any effective offertory. Many churches have tried to utilize the otherwise ugly procedure of taking up a collection for an expression of personal consecration. A scripture passage before the offering and a prayer following it comprise the simplest method of this attempt. I quote only two forms of consecration amongst those discovered as current usages. The first is in the form of a creed, taken from the service order of the Congregational Church of Webster Groves, Missouri. The second is from a special service arranged by the superintendent of the Chicago Southern District of the Methodist Episcopal Church.

Consecration of Offering.

I believe in the Fatherhood of God and in the Brotherhood of Man. I believe that Christ is the Way, the Truth and the Life. I believe in the clean heart, the unworldly mind and the service of love that Jesus taught and exemplified. I accept His spirit and His teaching.

Offertory Litany.

To the preaching of the good tidings of salvation
    We consecrate our gifts.
To the teaching of Jesus' way of life
    We consecrate our gifts.
To the healing of broken bodies and the soothing of fevered
      brows
    We consecrate our gifts.

To the leading of every little child to the knowledge and
love of Jesus

We consecrate our gifts.

To the caring for helpless age and the relief of all who
look to us for help

We consecrate our gifts.

To the evangelization of the city and the building of the
kingdom of God

We consecrate our wealth, our efforts and our lives.

It is of course true, for it could hardly be otherwise,
that the note of self-dedication finds expression in the
usual Communion Service of the Protestant bodies.
My impression is, however, that there is no very
clear consciousness of this element such as to lead to
its development as an important and specific part of
the service. There is likely to be a more definite recognition of the exercise of dedication in the more liturgical or fixed services. In the liturgy of King's
Chapel, Boston, is the following prayer taken from
the order for the Lord's Supper. It is a genuine expression of consecration.   52623

O Lord and Heavenly Father, we thy humble servants
earnestly desire thy fatherly goodness, mercifully to accept
this our sacrifice of praise and thanksgiving; beseeching
thee to grant that, looking unto Christ and entering into
the fellowship of his suffering, we may be changed into his
likeness and with him pass from death into life. And here
we offer and present unto thee, O Lord, ourselves, our
souls and bodies, to be a reasonable, holy, and living sacrifice unto thee; humbly beseeching thee, that all we who are
partakers of this holy communion may be filled with thy

grace and heavenly benediction. And although we be unworthy, through our manifold sins, to offer unto thee any sacrifice, yet we beseech thee to accept this our bounden duty and service; not weighing our merits, but pardoning our offences, according to thine abundant mercies in Christ Jesus our Lord; through whom all honor and glory be unto thee, O Father Almighty, world without end.

Amen.

In the published order for the Communion Service according to the use of the First Parish Church of Cambridge, Massachusetts, the minister speaks the following words in the administration of the sacrament:

In communion with the spirit of Jesus, and in behalf of this congregation, receive this cup of blessing; that it may be to us all a renewed pledge of that discipleship which is not in word alone, but in spirit and in truth.

The communion office prepared by the Reverend Harvey J. Loy for a Unitarian church contains a double oblation according to the ancient usage of the church.

THE OFFERTORY:

Accept, O Holy Father, Almighty and eternal God, this bread, which we offer thee from among thine own gifts in token that thou art the source of all our food, both earthly and heavenly; and grant that it may help us to come nearer to thee in the spirit.　　　　　Amen.

May we live in thy love, and fail not to receive thy benefits with grateful heart.　　　　　Amen.

We offer thee the fruit of the vine, that our thoughts and deeds, like it, may bring a sweet savor before thy presence.
Amen.

Pray, brethren, that our offering may be acceptable to God the Father Almighty.

PEOPLE:

May the Lord receive our offering, to the praise and glory of his name, unto our benefit, and that of all his holy church. Amen.

THE GREAT OBLATION:

Wherefore, O Lord and heavenly Father, we, thy humble servants, do celebrate and offer here before thee, of thine own gifts, this token of our sonship to thee and of our brotherhood with each other, even as thy servant Jesus did with his disciples. And together with this token, we offer the sacrifice of our thanksgiving and the incense of our prayers.

PREPARATION OF THE COMMUNICANTS:

And here, O most holy Father, we would present ourselves, our souls and bodies, to be a reasonable, holy, and living sacrifice unto thee; and we pray that, as this bread was once scattered on the mountains, and is here gathered into one, so thy children of every nation, kindred, and tongue, may be made one living and holy church; and as this wine was gathered from the fruit of the vine, so all thy people may abide as branches of that holy vine reaching up unto thee, and may bring forth good fruit to thy glory.

It will be observed that these communion prayers are adaptations of older material from the Prayer Book. They are so well done, however, as to justify the procedure, and well illustrate a legitimate method of rearranging or modifying older expressions. The Common Service Book of the Lutheran Church designates as The Offertory, scriptural sentences expressive of dedication.

The sacrifices of God are a broken spirit:
  A broken and a contrite heart, O God, Thou wilt not despise.
Do good in Thy good pleasure unto Zion:
  Build Thou the walls of Jerusalem.
Then shalt Thou be pleased with the sacrifices of righteousness:
  With burnt-offering and whole burnt-offering.

It would seem strange that the Lutheran Liturgy of Communion contains no offering of the material elements or no great oblation comparable to the usage of other liturgical bodies, not even comparable to the practice of some Unitarian parishes. The Offertory quoted, however, is used in the ordinary service of worship, and it should be remembered that in the Lutheran view several of the exercises of the ordinary service are regarded as sacrificial or dedicatory elements.

The fixing of purposes and perseverance in them is so vital to religion that it needs more and better forms of expression. I have no special wisdom in the matter for the ordinary service of worship. For the Communion Service I commend a fresh study of the older liturgies at this point, and the definite inclusion of an exercise of consecration brought into connection with the outer symbols of the sacrament.

PEACE

After the great adventure of the spirit in worship there remains a mood of composure which finds expression in the older liturgies. The effort of retreat to find the harmony and integrity of sanctuary, followed by the multiplicity of recollection, reordered by the achievement of purpose, should leave in the heart and mind a new self-possession as the steps return from the church to practical life. In the most of our free church services this is given expression in the closing hymn and a brief benediction. Possibly this is sufficient for the ordinary Sunday morning service of worship. At other times there may well be a more ample account of this phase of experience. To indicate the older usage I quote three brief Post Communion prayers from the Roman missal.

Grant, we beseech Thee, O Almighty God, That we may attain by the understanding of a purified mind that which we celebrate with solemn rite. Through Our Lord.

Being fed with celestial delights, we beseech Thee, O Lord, That we may ever hunger after those things by which we truly live. Through Our Lord.

Grant, we humbly beseech Thee, Almighty God, That those whom Thou refreshest with Thy sacraments may serve Thee worthily by a life well pleasing to Thee. Through Our Lord.

From a vesper service arranged for the Park Congregational Church of Norwich, Connecticut, is taken this beautiful closing exercise of the character indicated.

Prayer.

Prevent us, O Lord, in all our doings with thy most gracious favor, and further us with thy continual help; that in all our works begun, continued, and ended in thee, we may glorify thy holy Name, and finally by thy mercy obtain everlasting life; Through Jesus Christ our Lord.

CHOIR—Amen.

Ascription.

Now unto him that is able to do exceeding abundantly above all that we ask or think, according to the power that worketh in us, Unto him be glory in the church by Christ Jesus throughout all ages, world without end.

CHOIR—Threefold Amen.

Benediction.

Beloved, let your going forth be in the name of the Lord, and be ye thankful.

The grace of our Lord Jesus Christ be with you all.

CHOIR—Amen.

CHAPTER IV

The Aesthetics of Structure

Of the aesthetic attitude—It comes in helpful pulses in the more strenuous enterprises, as we stop in climbing great mountains to gather not only breath and refreshment, but the charm and magnificence that each fresh *étape* reveals. From time immemorial men have dedicated them as festivals, and solemn concourses. . . . Indeed, this is the definition of drudgery, the blind production of goods, cut off from all interpretation of their common enjoyment. . . . It has been the inspiration of universal religions, of political democracy, and later of industrial democracy to bring something of the universal achievement, of the solemn festival, of common delight into the isolated and dreary activities which all together make possible the blessed community, the state, the co-operative society, and all the meanings which we vaguely call social and spiritual.

GEORGE H. MEAD

IV.

THE setting and scene for the customary celebration of religion is the church building. Of all the arts that of architecture is the most pervasive because it touches everybody. The stuff of the earth is fashioned into forms capable of giving shelter for all the children of men. A large proportion of mankind has made some attempt to fashion these forms in such modes as are pleasing to the eye. Amongst all the buildings in the world the most significant and fascinating are the houses of prayer. A very quiver of ecstasy, compact of humility and joy, as that of Mary receiving the announcing angel, must be the sense of any man called upon to mold the shapes that are to house his fellow men for their supreme experience. The forms must be plain yet so ordered and subtle as to start the motions of life, simple yet rich with manifold intimations for the imagination.

Those who have followed our brief course of thought will have taken note of a recurring suggestion which has both limited and defined its scope. We have at all times kept before us the alternating character of the mystic life, its ceaseless journeys into the world, its perpetual retreat toward God. Celebration is a process of recollection brought to its fullest meaning in a moment of realization. In celebration, events are remembered, but remembered according as they are seen to have been of high moment in the total life. In that supreme celebration which rises to the nature of religion, the recollective process becomes universal and the total life presented is not only man's but God's. My present thought is that the church building may assist both the process of recollection and the joy of realization. It may minister the sense of totality in which all several things are merged and yet find their several worths. If the alternation of attention between the One and the many pervades the liturgy, so also it may pervade the church building.

First, it is the power of unification that we most value in religious structure. It is the sense of retreat and of sanctuary which calls for the most complete powers of the artist builder. How shall he devise those proportions, lights and shadows, shapes and surfaces which shall afford refuge and start the motions of integrity? How shall he cut away all other clamoring impulses save the search for God? How shall he eliminate all other concerns and affairs? How shall he effect distance, aloofness, withdrawal? How shall he suggest that supreme worth for which the world is well lost? I do not know just how he is to do these things, but I do believe that he should attempt them, for men desire refuge and sanctuary, and the touch of that which the world cannot give nor take away. Certainly, first of all the builder must conceive the possibility and the desirability of intimating these things in the structure itself. We cannot be satisfied with churches which are merely places of assembly, auditoriums, halls, when there are in the world and may again be in the world buildings which

in themselves minister the presence of divinity and
startle the human spirit to an awareness of it.

I make no doubt that in the technique to be utilized
to these ends, there must be that which makes an immediate or sensuous appeal. The building itself may
initiate that physical motion which vitalizes the beholder and rises into imaginative vigor. There are
many artistic possibilities of motion and of rhythm.
This is one of the chief reasons for the immemorial
use of the arcade or colonnade in religious structures.
These are powerful forms of rhythm, one of the essential qualities in all the great arts. Other and more
refined phases of the structural composition, flutings,
moldings, mullionings, abstract patterns and repetitive shapes may be arranged for their rhythmic value.
By the movement of the eye from point to point of
an arcade, by the stimulus to motion that is ever present in the horizontal lines of a nave and by the lure
of the high light or dominant centrality in the inte-
rior composition, the worshiper is disposed to move.
To move where? I hesitate to answer. At least I must
first remind you that no speech can exaggerate the potencies of beauty, the unutterable desire for life
which it awakens, the unmeasured promise of life
which it declares. I say, then, that he is disposed to
move not merely in body but in spirit, out of his present into his possible self, out of all things that are
into all that may be. He is quite literally disposed to
move toward God and to move on and on with God.

The selection and disposition of color is another of

the artist's opportunities in his effort to quicken ap-
prehending attention. If it be true that the heart of
man is made suddenly glad by the sight of pale green
water beyond the dark shore foliage of a northern
lake, or surprised into delight by the sapphire blue of
a southern sea, it need not decline to be pleased by the
translucent color of a gracious window or the warm
riches of a fresco or the magnificent glow of a glass
mosaic. All critics of the arts know the tendencies of
the primary colors to induce definite moods. I recall
at the moment the bluish light of a lady chapel in
New York, a very mass and volume of light, power-
fully suggestive of sanctuary; and also the golden
glow of a certain large side chapel where light comes
lavishly through amber windows, wooing the spirit
out of isolation. By the legitimate use of color the
physical pulses are moved, the mind is led away from
dullness and fatigue and the heart is persuaded that
there is goodness and grace in life, the life of all
things, because that goodness and grace are here instantly realized.

The religious artist must know and utilize the
power of proportion, the relations of length and
breadth and height. The living-room in your house is
likely an apartment some nine or ten feet high, and
possibly thirty feet long. It is an agreeable space to
be in. But supposing you were introduced into a vast
hall two or three hundred feet in length and half as
wide but the ceiling of which had only the ten foot
elevation of your drawing-room. You can readily
imagine the stifling effect. Such a room would of

course be absurd, but it suggests at once the effect of proportion. In a general way, the present tendency in church building in the matter of proportion is to increase length and height. Adventure and freedom are suggested by the sense of movement and space derived from these proportions. The more nearly square space fails to suggest movement and thus inhibits adventure. The ordinary rectangular American church is not a very brave form. It has not the assurance of the finished order of the Greek buildings, nor the bold quest of the Gothic.

Which brings us to the matter of style. Style in architecture is similar to style in literature. It is a problem of language itself. There are some who can speak the Gothic language and some who cannot. I am reminded of the swift remark of a very keen critic when someone proposed emphasizing the entrance façade of a plain building by a composition of superimposed classic orders. "Oh," he said, "you wish to say to everybody 'See, I know Latin.' " He was evidently one of those who feel that we should attempt to develop our own architectural language. Just at this moment the larger part of our church building is derived from the Gothic. Instead of beginning with the classic speech as the basis of development, it is using Gothic terms, but using them in combinations which amount almost to a new style. One might say that our Gothic diction differs from the old Gothic as our spoken language differs from Elizabethan speech. When we shall have moved forward as far as our speech is from Chaucer, we shall have achieved our own style. The popularity of Gothic means that many do not find satisfaction in the round arch, the line of which is turned back upon itself by the horizontal architrave. In the pointed arch there is less limitation to the upward sweep of vertical lines.

Meanwhile, we have not mastered the influence of our new materials, steel and concrete. The use of steel in small buildings dictates the horizontal line, in large structures it requires vertical expression. The arch which is necessitated in masonry structure becomes not a structural but only a reminiscent form when used in a steel building. It is for this reason in part that many are pleased that the best Gothic builders have revived the mighty mode of pure masonry building. There is a vibrant organism and technical excellence throughout a structure sustained by pure masonry which helps at once to destroy shams and to inspire a high integrity of life. Coherence of structure when achieved in stone is the more inspiring because of the difficulties of the accomplishment. My own feeling is that masonry structure is the best architectural language of religion, however much we may develop our own terms and phrases in new details that will at length give us our own style.

A corollary of masonry structure is the solution of the problem of surface. A masonry wall may be devised in larger areas than any other plain surface without being dead. It requires no tricks or slight devices to give it life. Inasmuch as extensive plain surfaces are otherwise valuable, as assisting the simplicity and composure of a great building, large or small, it is especially desirable that those surfaces do not at the same time convey a feeling of coldness or deadness. A building too much cluttered with details, either necessary details of windows, doors and structural parts, or details of ornamentation, induces restlessness by its excessive diversity. Many of the surface problems as well as the profound values of structure itself are solved by the adoption of masonry building. Calm repose and steadfast endurance of spirit are induced by a beautiful wall, laid up true and strong of clean stones. No thin cracking stucco nor wash of paint, no veined slabs of costly marbles recall the soul to honesty and perseverance as does a wall of stone or even for that matter a wall of the plainest brick or hard cement.

These elements of shapes and lines, surfaces and colors, proportions and rhythms and other arrangements of light and dark and mass, together with symbolic detail, comprise the resources of the builder's technique. These he must merge and harmonize by the total unity of his composition. Restraint and balance, elimination, subordination, relativity and other canons he must exercise with skill if he is to accomplish that supreme integration which it is his chief purpose to intimate. If there be no successful integration in the structure, it cannot assist the worshiper to find himself or to find the One he has come to seek. I do not mean to say that it is always the total harmony of the building which aids the spirit to the achievement of harmony. Sometimes one of the lesser parts, the shape of a pillar, the moldings of the soffits of an arch, the charming grace of flowing, melting lines and subtle shadows in a carved pulpit or reredos, absorb the attention, initiate motions of sympathy, or more accurately empathy, and so start the worshiper on a course of imaginative contemplation in which at last all things are ordered, all things fall into their appointed places in the mystery of the all embracing life. Yet also oftentimes it is not one particular phrase of the architectural symphony which leads the soul to contemplation and life but the total effect of the whole. The first of the canons of form in architecture, as in the other arts, is the law of unity.

If there is One whom we seek, then surely that which helps us to be rid of discords within helps us to find Him. If it is One that we seek, whatever aids us to compose all the outer confusions of our days helps us to find Him. If there is being and life flowing through all things, that which enlivens us in body and in mind communicates that life to us. So also, conversely, if all the artists that ever were have gathered into order and harmony the stuff of their forms it is because some inner conviction of order has urged them on. If there is a passion for composition in the human spirit, forever annoyed by discord, forever seeking peace within and without, ever taking delight in the great arts, it is born of an ineradicable feeling that there is One to be found. The church building then must itself be a work of art. Whatever may be its practical uses, whatever be the content of its symbolic teachings, its chief value will ever be the unifying mediation of its form. It is the scene of celebration, it is the place of joy, it is the setting for worship, it is the house of God.

Before taking leave of our attention to the church building as a unifying value, and making some note of its recollective suggestiveness, there are two or three other remarks to be made about symbols which relate to its worth for the festal side of celebration.

First, the one chief symbol of both artistic and religious unification in religion has always been the altar. It does not require the sacrifice of bullocks or of goats to validate the building of an altar. The sacrifice of thanksgiving and the sacrifice of contrite hearts is the true and spiritual sacrifice that is acceptable. The physical objectivity of the altar as a symbol of the inner and spiritual sacrifice tends to draw forth the offering. Before the altar of God men have always come confessing their weakness and need and so also with thankful hearts dedicating their strength. I must admit as readily as anyone that there is no adequate symbol of divinity, yet I believe that even a small and otherwise barren hall in which men have placed an altar is thereby set apart as a place of prayer and thereby enriched with intimations of holiness and sanctuary and divine life.

Artistically, no other device has been invented, and one might dare to say nor can be, so effective as the altar as the dominating centrality which gives unity to the entire work of structural art. It is the only satisfying solution for the point of focal attention to which all other lines and shapes lead. It is a fact of great significance that more and more Protestant

churches are realizing this. In almost all denomina-
tions, in liberal parishes as well as conservative, there
are already numbers of recent church buildings which
have adopted this great historic symbol of religion.
In every such instance of which I have heard, the
people have been stirred and gratified, the spirit of
devotion has been increased and the services of worship have been improved. The possibilities of helpful
worship are much increased by the adoption of the
traditional chancel plan of building, where also the
choir can be disposed about the altar and share the
service as the Greek chorus shared the movement of
the drama. It is less easy in such a building for the
people to comport themselves in an irreverent manner or for the minister to conduct a slovenly service
of worship. Reverence is enhanced and the whole
tone of worship elevated in a building that is unmis-
takably devoted to religion.

The next remark is in some ways a more difficult
one, but worthy of notice. It is that in some strange
way a building not used has lost a part of its religious
value, whereas signs of human presence increase the
sense of divinity. If all that has been said about the
influence of the arts and the power of a noble church
building to foster the religious experience be true,
human presence or absence would seem inconsequential. Many will recall the soaring lines and lofty
vaults together with the splendor of ancient glass in
Sainte Chapelle at Paris, standing unimpaired. But
much of the life has gone out of the building because
religious rites are no longer performed in it. Perhaps

the sharp regret for such a situation tends to stifle the values which still inhere in the great structure, because when the ruin of a building has passed beyond the possibility of repair the artistic effect of its fragments may be very powerful. The Cistercian abbeys and the few groups of Greek columns still standing rouse us to the keenest aesthetic appreciation. The Protestant church building loses a great part of its value because there is nothing to invite the presence of the devotee or to indicate that he has lately come and gone. A church with an altar is better furnished with ever present invitation and welcome to private devotions than an auditorium. People have no habit of coming into our churches not only because they are locked up but also because there is nothing to suggest their coming excepting for public occasions. Many individual Protestant parishes have long since realized this and established the custom of the ever open door in the church. Whether the altar is used as the central object of interest or not, the church building should be so composed as to invite visitation and offer its total message at all times. In this connection, it is most fortunate if the floor spaces of the building do not need to be entirely occupied by seats. If one or more passages or aisles or chapels can be left clear of pews, there is space to wander about in. If, moreover, there are works of art in bas-relief or fresco, wood or glass, these serve to give life to the building and a rich experience to the visitor. But reminders of human presence are important also. Fresh flowers upon an altar or in the vestibule indicate life and welcome.

The older mode of indicating daily life in the house
of God is the use of lights. Altar candles and sanctuary lamps directly declare to the worshiper that he
has been expected. Many Jewish congregations still
retain the use of the altar lamp. Probably few Protestants would care to revive the custom of the individual placing of little candles at shrines in a church.
Yet when you see them in an old church you know
that a worshiper has recently passed that way.

The outside of a church building is important as
well as the inside. I have in mind now not so much
the artistic success of the structure as to line, mass and
balance of composition but rather its success as a symbol of religion in the midst of the community. The
church spires in the village and the cathedral towers
of the old cities are adequate symbols of the place of
religion in life. It is growingly difficult in modern
cities to provide for any comparable prominence for
the house of worship. The size of modern structures
on the one hand and sectarian divisiveness on the
other have resulted in the comparative insignificance
of religious structures. In my own city, we are building a three million dollar aquarium and projecting a
ten million dollar museum of commercial art, but
there is only one church structure in the entire city
suitable to a metropolitan situation. I cannot here
argue the case but only express a conviction that we
should have and could have one or more cathedrals
to stand as a perpetual call to worship and afford a
proper setting for the grand function of worship in
the civic life. We live in a time when many leaders in

the arts and sciences and many masters of commerce have grown up without having had much contact with liberal religion. Our spiritual culture is divided and confused. Religion has always been the informing, pervading power in the development of matured culture. It can hardly be otherwise in times to come. It is just possible that bold projects for structures symbolic of the presidency of religion would go far toward the achievement of the cultural unity we now lack. Where there are no individual parish bodies of sufficient strength to provide such a structure, several religious societies might combine in a form of collective or collegiate organization for this purpose. Such a form of organization would not only make possible a more imposing building but would itself achieve the more broadly civic and cultural character many desire to see assumed by religion.

The church building, then, is first of all valuable for the celebrative life of religion. It calls us from work to worship, it helps us forget the many and consider the One, it ministers totality, in its harmony and wholeness it stands for God.

The celebration of life is not only a festal occasion of worship but the remembrance of work. It is not only the joy of present harmony and fullness of life, but recollection. That recollection is not merely the memory of all things that have gone before but the survey of all things that are to be expected or desired or attempted. The religious experience is always the song of the great rhythm of God and man; the retreat from the world, the return to the world; the

vision of the One, the recollection of the many; sacramental reception of grace, sacrificial dedication to
toil.

The church building itself may assist the process of
recollection as well as the process of retreat. It may
be not only sanctuary but also meeting house and civic
home. The mediaeval church was rich in many kinds
of symbolic teaching. The building was a grand com-
posing harmony calling the spirit away from the
world, offering repose and peace and refreshment by
its structural forms, but it offered also definite mental and moral content through the symbolisms of innumerable decorative details. The history and the
dogmas of the faith were set forth in carved wood
and stone, painted glass, tapestries and frescoes in all
parts of the church. Excepting for a meager and not
very artistic use of painted windows, Protestantism
has made little use of the church building as a means
of suggesting the recollective content of religion. Today there are the beginnings of a widespread realization of a great opportunity in the symbolism of the
church building.

On the whole, it might be said that religion has
never yet fully grasped the logic of the recollective
process, and hence never fully symbolized it in the
arts. It has always emphasized the corporate character
of its own life and symbolized the wider communion
of the saints. Its recollection has corrected the vagaries
of individual piety, but has never adequately caught
up the great normal concerns of practical life nor the
joys and sorrows of creative toil. To be sure, there

are the plowman of Giotto and other toilers on the great tower in Florence. And in the Spanish Chapel, coupled with the Virtues sit the Sciences. So also to-day, the renewed interest in symbolism thus far is manifested in ways which broaden the communion of saints with only here and there a recollection of the practical life. Yet even this distinctively religious symbolism is a very recent interest amongst the free churches. In the last Gothic church that I have per-sonally visited there are suggestive symbols every-where, quiet, tasteful, thoroughly subdued by the large scale of the structure, but vivid reminders of many things broad and deep in the story of human faith, the pelican, the star, the anchor, the crowned rose, the fish, the labarum, the cross. Seven corbels represent seven historic epochs, the seven-branched candlestick for the Hebrew church, the lamb for the early Christian age, IHS for triumph, the shield for the Crusader, the monk for monasticism, the Bible for the Reformation, the Mayflower for aspira-tion. As a new sign and symbol of this particular parish, there is carved a cross with three interlocking circles representing the brotherhood of man and the inclusive community church ideal. The new chapel now building at the University of Chicago will be adorned with symbolic plastics, the most of them recollective of religious development. The jambs of the great window of the entrance façade will recall the Te Deum by figures of apostles, prophets and martyrs. The frieze across the gable will be com-posed of heroic figures sketching the march of reli-

gion, beginning with Abraham and following through
to Reformation times. Zoroaster and Plato are the
non-Christian heroes represented. For various reasons, in other parts of the building will be demi-
figures of two University presidents and two stu-
dents, two American statesmen, two poets, a musician
and an architect. These serve to broaden the scope of
religious experience. In addition to these representations of individual persons, all connected with the
history of religion, there will be four prominent symbolic figures representing four categories of human
interest, the artist, the philosopher, the scientist and
the statesman.

One of the most interesting of recent symbolic
works in lovely carved wood is the Shippen pulpit in
the Unitarian church of Lancaster, Pennsylvania.
The figures represent religious liberators, Borrhaus,
Servetus, David, Socinus, Lindsey, Channing, Mar-
tineau, Hale, Collyer, and Père Hyacinthe. In the
same church there is the beginning of that wider outreach toward which we are moving. A scientist, a me-
chanic and a merchant are symbolically represented
in the carvings of the lectern.

In a recent design for a reredos, there are included
figures of Printer and Writer, Builder, Scientist,
Statesman and Philosopher, with the familiar coup-
let;

Let us now praise famous men
Even the artificer and work-master.

You will see that I am seeking to suggest what

may be possible in a church building to assist the worshiper in his process of recollection by simple but
definitely symbolic representations. Moreover, I am
seeking to suggest that they represent not only the
history of religious life but also the story of common
life. To do this without the risk of fixing usages
which should be fluid is difficult, yet I believe it can
be done. One of the best categorical selections for
symbolic representation of which I have heard is the
ideal career of man as worked out in the church
school building of St. John's Reformed Church at
Lansdale, Pennsylvania. A series of medallions in
beautiful leaded glass carry the scheme through the
several departments of the school. The plan is richly
suggestive of new and vigorous developments in the
religious arts. In the Kindergarten room, two medallions portray the Sheepfold and the Lamb in the
Crib. For the Beginners there are nature symbols—
Air, Earth, Sky and Sea. The Primary Department
for children beginning their public school life has two
symbols, the Church Flag and the Nation's Flag. The
Juniors are taught the unity of life by representations
of their chief centers of life—the Home, the School,
the Playground and the Church. Intermediate pupils
are given two interesting symbols, the Greek Cross
and a Fork-in-the-Road, one to set forth the four-
fold ideal, the other emblematic of the choice of life.
The Young People's Department contains two pairs
of symbols. The Torch and the Sunrise represent the
past and the future. Liberty and law are symbolized
in a way to teach their relations. The Adult rooms

contain representations of the Open Bible and the Altar for religion and four symbols of work, the Artist, the Farmer, the Merchant and the Teacher bound by clasped hands and flowers. These works are simple and of small size though of rich materials. They will convey not merely the delight of beauty but also concrete teaching of great value.

I know of no Protestant church that has made the experiment I should like to see tried, as to both content and form. If we have long had the stained glass window, and are now moving rapidly toward the use of carved figures in wood and stone, I should like to see attempted also the painted fresco. If we are to have the advantages of austerity, restraint and structural coherence to be had in buildings of stone masonry, we must discover ways of adding warmth and color. As to the content of symbolic representations in color, I suggest the category of the world's work. The great poles of alternating life are worship and work. There are other ways of cataloging experience for the sake of understanding or management. Yet it would seem that all experience might be gathered under the descriptions of celebrative worship on holy days and common toil on ordinary days. If many different phases of the world's work could be symbolized on the walls of the church aisles, these frescoes would serve many profound purposes. They would afford immediate delight according to their excellence as works of art. They would teach the morals of productivity, inspire the worshiper to emulation and achievement. They would give direction to the urgencies of creativity born in the mystic experience. They would acknowledge and celebrate the mutual interdependence of all men. They would offer a concrete content for the recollective experience of the worshiper. Worship is the forgetting of work, release from the monotony of irksome labor, withdrawal and unification. But it is also the remembrance of work. The mystic way is a path forth and back. Its course is not complete without the return to responsibility. Indeed, the One whom we seek cannot be the One whom we need unless all separate things also are found in Him. Indeed, no separate thing is found until it is found in Him. The oneness we seek is that which comprehends all things. It cannot be easily or cheaply apprehended. The joy of the celebration is not joy at all if we must return to disorder and separation. Its very joy is the joy of finding the import of our affairs composed in the grand design of the divine life.

It is this essential character of worship itself which requires at its very heart the recollection of affairs, the rearrangement of their importance and the reconsecration of the self to them. I sympathize with the intelligent woman who objected to my project for frescoes of the world's work on the ground of her desire for sanctuary. I should be the last to propose anything that would lessen the value of the church building as a place of refuge and of communion with God, yet the very integrity of that communion involves a reappraisal of the active life as also a concern for the divine life. Protestant sermons have never been lacking in moral urgencies. Ethical earnestness is the glory of American religion. But there is much ethical idealism dissevered from the religion of the church because we have failed to bring the world's work into the celebrations of religion. Our ethical discussion has been serious but not always happy. If we could gather special groups of toilers, hand workers and brain workers to offer definite praise for what they do for us all in their daily life of productivity, we should not only assist them to a nobler conception of the total worth of their labor but also be better circumstanced to suggest improvements in the ideals of industry. The gathering of such groups would be made the easier and the happier if they might be invited to a church building where the dignities of toil were always upheld in portrayals of agriculture and mining, commerce and poetry and all the labors of man. And how natural on these occasions to make them bright festivals by a processional of minister and choristers to conduct a portion of the service from the chapel representing the work especially celebrated.

Many needed values might be discovered by a bold experiment such as I have sketched. Here is a way to regain the festal note in religion neither bizarre nor artificial. Here is a way to recover the decorative riches of the church without meaningless revivals. Here is a way to connect religion with daily life, interesting and vital. Here is a form adequate to give carrying power to the big content of modern humanistic ethics. Here is a way to bring into the church, if only occasionally, many men, perhaps whole classes of men, not now related to specific religion. Here is a way for the church to regain the leadership of culture, that total societal culture which is both good taste in the arts and noble disposition in all the relations of life.

I am well aware of the artistic difficulties of symbolic art. The art critics do not much approve works which begin in concepts. But religion has used symbolic art extensively in the past and may do so again. Those who would hesitate to use the strong notes of the painted fresco might attempt quieter works, such as carvings in wood. Some of the finest wood carving in the world has been done in America within the last decade, and much more of it than most of us are aware of. Compositional works in glass are now being rendered with a mastery of that medium comparable to the best of mediaeval artistry. Here and there in America are parishes which long for the infinitely gracious beauty of decorative and symbolic forms wrought with painstaking and loving care such as we have been taught once characterized the craftsmanship of olden times. And they will achieve their desires. There is already well under way a revival of interest in the religious arts which will soon make the churches of America the outstanding art centers of the land. It is good to collect precious bits of the old ecclesiastical arts in our great museums. But also it seems a strange blindness that some have, who cherish a few crumbling fragments of a once brilliant art without being aware that we might again have, indeed are already beginning to have, a new and living religious art of our own.

The religious structure, then, is at once the scene and symbol of the supreme experience of life. As a work of art its effect is that of pure form. The primary aesthetic appeal of the building contains no specific content of ideas, it is the appeal of mass, line, proportion, rhythm and other formal elements of structural art. Its own coherence tends to induce harmony in the same elemental way as any other work of art, and to satisfy the deeper thirst of human nature for order in the self and in the world. When to this aesthetic appeal is added the known fact that the building stands for the idea of order, for worship, for God, its unifying effect becomes very powerful. But the very desire for unity is born of our everyday experience with many forms of mutiplicity. We do not crave a unity which forgets that diversity but which composes and harmonizes it. Into the church must be brought the discord and distractions, the duties and pleasures we desire to have unified. There in the worship of the church, the events and ideas recollected are rejected or praised according to their total significance, according to their import in the light of all things. In the celebration of life nothing is ignored, it is life entire and complete that is loved and praised.

The church building affords the most favorable conditions for this celebrative achievement. It assists the soul on its retreat toward sanctuary and God. It may assist also the return to the world. It may con-

tain such symbolic representations as shall recall the
worshiper to his work. If worship is the celebration of
life, it must be rich in a content recollective of the
goods of all days as well as the good of holy day.
The abiding form of celebration, the one eternal order of God is filled with the ever moving content of
all things old and new. Worship as the celebration of
life is the active love and praise of all the life there
is, the love and praise of God.

CHAPTER V

Problems in Contrast

There are at present no indications that the great bulk of non-liturgical churches in America are likely to develop liturgies in the near future. The tradition of the freer service is very strong, and the American temperament requires occasion for informality and initiative. There is probably a principle at stake here, which may not be too easily relinquished. But the present fact is that the original truth of the free service has become in practice a rather uninspired and uninspiring platitude.

WILLARD L. SPERRY

There is a kind of worship which is perfectly objective and sincere and that is quite as possible for the intelligent man of to-day as it was for the ancient:—namely that union of awe and gratitude which is reverence, combined perhaps with consecration and a suggestion of communion, which most thoughtful men must feel in the presence of the Cosmic forces and in reflecting upon them.

JAMES BISSETT PRATT

V.

MANY baffling problems occur and recur to those who are concerned with the conduct of public worship. The most of these take the form of contrasting principles. Some of them were given very scant attention in the four original lectures. Others were omitted entirely as not falling easily into the schematic plan chosen. I believe that the most of them are at least partially solved by the formulas set forth in the lectures. A more specific word about some of them might be valuable.

The problem of formality and informality has not yet been faced by the evangelical churches. The type of worship service to which the typical American Protestant is accustomed is essentially informal. It uses fixed forms, doxologies, prayers, anthems, psalms, and other recurring materials, but the management of the forms has been informal. The minister has been so little the priest and so much the preacher, so little the functionary and so largely a person, that his conduct of the service is highly individual. Our great congregations have gathered round interesting and magnetic personalities. Without being immodest, though many have been that, these men have not been gifted in self-effacement or mergence in the process of their religious acts. Big-voiced, eloquent men accustomed to moving numbers of people by the arts of rhetoric and the vigor of personal magnetism simply do not know how to moderate themselves to the larger rhythms of a more objective worship. It is a little difficult, sometimes, to put your finger on just this or that inflection of voice, unnecessary remark or subtle attitude which constitutes a personal intrusion. Yet I have oftentimes observed it. Many of the best denominational preachers do not know how to conduct a formal service of worship because they cannot keep themselves out of it. They are like the golf players who cannot be rid of the fault of pressing the ball. The good golfer knows that the right form will itself do the work. The proper club swung properly will lift the ball. No extra intrusive pressing is required. It is precisely so with a liturgy. Not that the spirit or emotion of the minister makes no difference. But the spirit and emotion must be so merged into the technique of the form selected that they are not obtrusive. There are very great values to be enjoyed from the personal conduct of worship. There are men who can come into a gathering of worshipers, large or small, and lift the people toward God in the most simple and immediate way as they offer prayers, announce hymns and speak the direct word of exhortation. It would be an irreparable loss if this gift of the spirit should be quenched. It is a gift through which many wonderful aspects of evangelical piety have been developed and nurtured. But it is a highly subjective and erratic gift. More and more people today are unsatisfied not with the occasions when the gift succeeds but with the far larger number of occasions when it fails of operation. There is an increasing desire for the more dependable quality of objective and impersonal worship.

It is always difficult to estimate tendencies of the times, because almost every major movement has its countercurrents. Moreover, both current and counter-current in one region are affected by movements of another character altogether. In noting the actuality of a widespread desire for improvement in worship, and a renewed interest in liturgical forms of worship, it is fair to note opposite influences also. There are typical evangelical church leaders who are aware of a rising liturgical interest but who dislike and oppose it. They rightly fear the loss of some important values in their modes of expression. There are certain religious radicals to whom any sort of traditional form is disagreeable. The values cherished by both of these parties are important. The temper of evangelical piety is a vital force, keeping always fresh the spirit of evangelism and revival. The free-minded pursuit of the truth is no less necessary to the vitality of religion. There is nothing to fear from the discoveries of truth. There is something to fear, however, from the bad religious psychology and the crudity which radicals often manifest and there is much that is wanting in the evangelical temper as the only spiritual outlook.

Neither of these parties is sufficient for the future. The one is the large body of American Protestantism, the other a small but energetic group of admirable progressives. Curiously enough, both suffer the same difficulty, both typify the immaturity of American religion. The usages and customs of evangelicalism still retain a character derived from the frontier. The

free and easy informality of pioneer life has not yet
disappeared from many religious societies. In some
churches one feels as though the tentative and tempo-
rary makeshifts of the early days had been crystal-
lized. Indeed, it is true of all Protestantism that it
has never entered an adequately constructive stage,
that it still lives upon a comparatively narrow range
of modes and methods and forms of expression. Of
certain religious radicals it is noteworthy that they
have reacted against the intellectual weaknesses of
frontier religion without themselves being in possession of that culture which might have led them to re-
act also against the cultural meagerness of the evangelical system.

So despite both these countercurrents, there is a
strong tide of desire for deeper experience and better
forms in worship. Unfortunately, perhaps, the sense
of need for better forms sometimes outruns the development of the deeper experience. For instance,
there are numbers of new churches and academic
chapels built in a style and arrangement of parts
which were originally developed for and still call for
some form of liturgical worship. But the people who
use them do not seem to know how to behave in their
own buildings. They have not previously developed
any exercises of devotion suitable for transfer to a
new building of the type constructed. They suffer the
dilemma of trying to conduct an informal type of
worship where it is out of place, without knowing
just how to develop that which is appropriate to their
new scene and setting. Yet these very buildings are a

testimony of dissatisfaction with the old methods. Possibly they will inspire deeper desires and assist in pointing the way toward the better day of which they are a presage. At any rate, no one can study the recent church architecture of America and deny a wide-spread change in the direction of nobler forms of worship.

There are already large numbers of people who find the shifting emotions of an individual minister a very undependable basis for the inspirations of worship. They are beginning to value the stable and objective character of a more formal liturgy. Others remain unmoved, if indeed they are not definitely annoyed by the literary ineptitudes of the average minister in his conduct of worship. They find refreshment in the vigor, variety and grace of better-prepared materials. Some are definitely aware that religion is not primarily intellectual, and they find only a thin and dry experience in most of the extremely liberal churches. Still others are weary of the sermon as the chief feature of the Protestant service. They are busy with ideas in many other connections and while they value thinking in religion, they wish also to find in church such large and capacious forms as may be favorable to the reorganization of their own ideas and to the enjoyments of vitality and peace. For all these classes of persons the typical evangelical service is no longer satisfying. In a general way, the fault which underlies all these difficulties is the excessive subjectivity of the informal mode of worship.

Which leads to the much discussed problem of the

subjective and objective phases of worship. As in the case of most dilemmas the logical limits of either choice lead to absurdities. Worship conducted without any end save the effect upon the congregation becomes self-conscious and fails to achieve the larger values sought. Purely objective worship, careless of participants or human influence, has never appealed to Protestantism. The dilemma is perhaps not a real one. In the older Christian rites the central and most sacred act of worship was the great oblation, originally the sacrifice of praise, thanksgiving and contrition. In later rituals the oblation became almost purely objective, an offering of external, corporeal elements. Even so, in most of the Eastern liturgies it scarce ever lacked vestiges of the idea of spiritual offering. In either case there is an intermixture of objective and subjective aspects. The more purely objective rite was performed in order to obtain the benefits of salvation. These benefits were often conceived in a crudely objective way. The great religious tradition, however, has always been a more spiritual one. The oblation, offered to an objective Other, was a spiritual, that is to say, a subjective offering, and the benefit desired was conceived as a real divine grace and gift, that is, objectively derived, yet conceived as a spiritual or subjective benefit. There is no valid objection of modern science or philosophy to such a conception of worship. There are religious objections to objective worship in its crude forms. There are both religious and psychological objections to purely subjective worship which takes no genuine account of some supreme object to which devotion is offered and from which grace is received. As has been suggested in the lecture on Celebration, and in the discussion of the pattern of worship, the nature of worship is an awareness of good, a recognition, a thanksgiving, an offering of rejoicing, followed by renewal and vitality. It is a great giving and a great receiving. It is ascent and return. I am now more than ever inclined to emphasize this double nature of worship, as offering and grace, as sacrifice and sacrament. There is a mighty and perhaps central value to be recovered in the conception and in the deed of the great oblation. Whether Protestantism might recapture the practice of going to church not to hear a sermon or "to be inspired," but to make an offering, is questionable. Sometimes it seems to me to be the one needed teaching and effort in this great matter.

In any case, the more formal and objective type of service is better for both sacrifice and sacrament. The genuine act of self-dedication, expressed in the jubilation of praise and thanksgiving and in some form of consecration can hardly be performed through the informalities of the more free services of worship. On the other hand, also, there is in a developed liturgic form a more solid and objective body as a sacramental vehicle of benefit. Something more substantial and objective than the average free church worship is called for by these and other considerations if our worship is to be more than an erratic and subjective exercise.

Another of the supposed problems of worship is

that of enrichment and simplicity. It is assumed by critics of liturgical worship that formality means enrichment and elaboration. In the best sense it does, but not primarily. On the contrary, the very first canon of good form is simplicity. No work of art is a work of art at all save as its multiformity is subdued and mastered by some strong and simple outline of easily apprehensible unity. A good service may be elaborate, but it must be simple; it may contain many treasures of enrichment, but they must be merged and ordered by a competent total form. The usual service should not be too rich or elaborate. Many informal services that I have observed are the most elaborate. Some are elaborate without being rich. In one church that I have in mind, the service takes twice as long as it should and has too many numbers. It is elaborate but informal. It is not so good as those which are simple but formal. If an enriched service is desired it can hardly avoid confusion and over-elaboration if informally conducted. It may be given simplicity by adequate care in the fashioning of its dominating forms and by strict adherence to a formal mode of conduct.

Enrichment, moreover, may be very desirable instead of undesirable. Religion has been defined by some as the abundant life, the ever expanding outreach to make connection with more and more aspects of reality. Far too often, and especially in evangelical circles, the religious experience which congregations of people have actually derived from the church has been a narrowing one rather than an increase of ap-

prehensions. Through other contacts and connections
many people develop a richer cultural experience, a
more adventurous life of thought and a more vital
share in the ethical endeavors of the day. To resume
the language of the lectures, the process of retreat
from the world has been emphasized but the recollective process has been little developed. Evangelical
Christianity is generally failing today at this point.
It has not brought the treasures of the arts and sciences into the recollective efforts of its worship. To
be sure, the sermon is the chief opportunity for this
enrichment, but not the only one. In the forms of
worship themselves must be found a place for reminders of all the major adventures of the spirit
which engage the interest and devotion of the people.
The process of collection and comprehension is of
little worth if there be only meager materials to be
surveyed. The process of retreat becomes cowardice
and failure and ignorance if it does not carry with it a
vivid awareness of many aspects of life. The struggle
for unity and harmony of life has little meaning if it
does not seek to master the genuine multiplicities
which people face. The enrichment which many desire in worship is not a mere matter of more sump-
tuous forms. It is rather an enlargement of the scope
of the mystic recollection. It is the remembrance of
more affairs and more values as well as the immediate
achievement of a wider range of values. This is one
of the opportunities of an improved lectionary. Instead of sermons which are little more than frames
for extensive literary quotations, it is better to use the

literary material frankly as scripture readings in the service of worship. I have already made in the fourth lecture a suggestion of method for extending and vivifying the recollective content of worship in the sphere of industry.

Another of the contrasts of worship today is that of specific or generic religion. It is a time of growing impatience with separatistic movements and of increasing knowledge of other historic lines of spiritual life than our own, no matter to which strain any of us may happen to belong. One does not need to see very far ahead to see that the prevalent desires for Protestant unity will grow into desires for religious unity. It is possible that we shall soon realize that we cannot permanently remain apart as separate religionists any more than we can remain separate denominationalists. Increasing occasions for spiritual fellowship are no longer confined to the bounds of Protestant Christianity. We are rapidly multiplying opportunities of contact with those of other faiths. Here we touch upon a vast world process far too large for discussion in this connection, yet it comes to our attention many times and in many ways and cannot be ignored. Almost within the lifetime of living men, many ancient races and nations have passed through drastic changes involved in the world-wide scope of commerce and the world-wide commonality of political ideas. This process of developing a world community of ideas and experience is moving forward with great rapidity. There are no longer any corners of the globe where major races are entirely unaware of cer-

tain leading aspects of modern life. To believe that
the usages of religion can escape this process is fatu-
ous. Some are glad to recognize it and to set their
course of action in line with it. They feel that the
time has come for modern religion to break away
from the existing bodies and form itself anew outside
the bounds of any historic religion. There is much to
say for such a course. It frees the worshiping community from embarrassing connections with the
overly conservative parties in the church. It stimu-
lates the imagination to fresh outlooks and new constructive formulations. It affords opportunity for
fellowship with those who have inherited other religious traditions. It permits the conservation of values
from various historic religions.

Meanwhile, however, there are some who regret
the loss of color, distinction, charm and variety of
life involved in the breakdown of ancient cultures. In
this great world process of enlarging interrelations,
they see a leveling down of life, a confusion of
values, a corruption of cultures, an impoverishment
of life. In the same way they rebel against the loss of
distinction and color involved in any movement of
syncretism or eclecticism in religion. Understanding
the profound relations of religion and culture, they
believe that it is neither possible nor desirable to develop the same culture or the same religion for the
entire human race. Indeed, there are already powerful countercurrents opposing the processes of eclecticism. The major racial and nationalistic movements
of the time are in large part economic and political,

but more profoundly they are also cultural. In India and in China, the politics of the West are more acceptable than Western culture and religion.

Many Chinese Nationalists do not wish to become Christians. They wish to revive the best elements in their most ancient religious and moral structures. Whatever they admire in Christianity they wish to graft upon their own native stock. They have no heart for any root and branch extermination of their own tree of life. But many Christians feel the same thing. Christianity also is a culture as well as a religion. Both as religion and culture it contains within itself ample vitalities for the sloughing off of outworn tissues and the putting forth of new buds of development.

From the point of view of spiritual continuity and wealth, it would seem to be far more desirable for the followers of Mahatma Gandhi to remain inside the ancient frame of the Hindu faiths than to come into formal fellowship with Christianity, or than, rejecting both, to seek a new eclectic formation. From precisely the same point of view, it would seem to be more desirable for those of us born in Christendom to remain inside the ancient frame of Christianity. A premature eclecticism defeats its own ends. Seeming to broaden the range of religious usage and experience, it rather narrows it. It cuts off without a sufficient period of testing and retesting, some of the most precious and beautiful religious treasures. It barters away the family heirlooms for the cheaper furniture that may happen to be the taste of a less mature life.

To maintain the historic continuity, on the other hand, and the present fellowship of the visible church, serves many deep and instinctive desires in the West as in the East, yet it does not answer also the equally powerful desires for change and growth unless the Christian churches are to be far more favorable to new development than they have been. For my own part, I should prefer to enter a church enriched by certain symbols of Christianity, and containing also symbolic reminders of other faiths, than to enter a building barren of historic acknowledgments of any kind. I believe that such a building would be the more gratefully entered by the devotee of an alien faith. Instead of casting out our Christian symbols, I should prefer to bring in others also. In parish churches with sufficient strength to erect buildings of large scale, there is opportunity for a Chapel of All Faiths. In cities where there are large alien populations such a chapel might frequently meet the needs of many strangers who have no other sanctuary. It might also serve to quicken and broaden the spiritual fellowship of the Christian congregation itself. The principle of specific religion is maintained, but modified to show respect for other specific faiths.

The same principle applies to the problem of the so-called community church. Hitherto the community church has developed its usages by a process of subtraction instead of addition. It has brought together various elements on the basis of some common denominator which has often proved to be a very slight foundation. My own conviction is that the *bona fide* community church must proceed by the method of addition. Any group of people with any kind of religious usage should be given a place in the actual community church. Instead of leaving out the particular forms and customs of differing groups, they should all be brought in. The true community church will be a place where the forms of worship are not restricted to the mediocrities of typical Protestantism, but rather enlarged to include the rites and customs of greatly divergent religious bodies.

Allied with this is the problem of personal or social religion. The strict logic of personal religion calls for no social worship whatever. The strict logic of social worship is theocracy, the complete mergence of church and state. The American consciousness has always assumed the separation of church and state as axiomatic. This view is derived not from the Reformation on the Continent but from the separatistic movement in England. The church is a body of believers, not the whole citizenship. Religion is an immediate and individual experience of God, not simply a comprehending organization of men. The celebrations of religion as expressed in the hymns and prayers of the church are largely the celebrations of personal salvation. This conception and practice has achieved two great values for religion, the genuineness of the experience and the depth or intensity of it. But it has also left outside the institutions of religion many people who cannot claim the experience. Nations which have maintained a state church have perhaps suffered some loss of depth in religious

experience, but they have gained in comprehensive-
ness. They could gain much more if they might more
completely pursue the logic of their choice. They are
well circumstanced to expand the conception of com-
prehensiveness to include the celebrations of many
aspects of life not now much noticed by religion.

I am thinking of this matter in some very concrete
ways. For instance, some large American universities
have recently abandoned required attendance on religious services. I believe they would not have done so
if we were not all so fixedly confirmed in the notion
of religion as strictly personal. If the faculty of a
great university had an imaginative concept of religion as a comprehending and societal category, the
logic of that concept would develop an academic
service of worship as the central feature of university
life. If we begin by assuming that religion is a purely
personal concern, supplemented by the assumption
that it is also specific and historic, then we eliminate
all those who cannot claim it for themselves person-
ally or who cannot agree to its specific form. If, on the
other hand, we assume that religion is the attempt of
an entire societal body to achieve the highest self-
consciousness and relational character of which it is
capable, then by very definition that religion must include all members of that particular society. At any
rate, I should like to see some great university make
the attempt to express itself as a whole in the highest
corporate manner, with the definite consciousness that
such expression may be and is religious.

In much the same way some American community

may in time have enough imaginative elements in it
to attempt a religious experiment from the societal
point of view rather than from the purely personal
and individual point of view. A group of groups will
be formed which will say to each other, We propose
to construct a religious body comprising all our concerns: we begin with no prejudicial notions of personal religious experience: we wish to bring together
all our affairs and seek to understand them, enjoy
them and direct them in the highest imaginable ways.
If some of those groups were typical Protestant
churches, then their cherished insights would be included in the whole. If some of the groups were
secular civic bodies their affairs also would be taken
account of.

I am not proposing a state church but a nobler and
more inclusive form of community church. In the
fourth lecture there is a suggestion of what any local
parish church might do to lift its religious experience
toward the character of a comprehending category.
It is of course true that churches have always attempted to attain something of this quality. The joys
and sorrows of all sorts and conditions of men and
now especially all sorts of social conditions are remembered in the church. No one can claim, however,
that any church of our time has been very highly successful in the vivid representation of the many aspects of life which are the concerns of the community. No one local religious body in the nature of the
case can be inclusive of many community concerns in
a concrete way. What I am trying to suggest here is

that in some communities it may be worth while to attempt the societal point of view in religion by a form of collective organization. I hope for the organization of collegiate churches, free cathedrals, where several religious bodies together with civic bodies will coöperate in a big experiment of societal religion. Some of the constituent churches might select to worship together, others would be assigned separate hours or separate chapels for their distinctive rites and usages. It would be eminently desirable if a considerable variety in forms of worship might thus be developed under the same roof. Such a plan would permit the conservation by any religious body of all its cherished principles and customs. It would permit any included church to coöperate with other organizations in developing newer forms of the celebration of life without having to abandon the separate enjoyment of its old forms.

In another place, I have more fully set forth the conception and possible plan of operation for an American cathedral.[1] Some such project is the only conceivable way to bring into the celebrations of religion all the actual concerns which ought to be included in them, and also to bring to the civic life that elevation and unity which cannot be achieved by anything less than religion. It would be the nearest approach to the state church possible to the genius of America. It would have no interest for those who are entirely satisfied with the conception of religion as purely private and personal, though it would in no

[1] *Century Magazine*, March, 1925.

way lessen the opportunities of such. It is the inevitable logic of development for all those who feel the weakness of private religion. It is the logic which ought to be considered in those countries which have a state church. If the French nation, which claims the ownership of its glorious mediaeval monuments as the possession of all the people, might open the doors of its great cathedrals for other rites as well as the Roman, such a procedure would signalize a new development of national culture and spiritual progress. The great Gothic aisles might again afford worthy setting for occasions of social solidarity and celebration. If our American cities could erect similarly noble structures, they too would provide opportunity not only for the gatherings of small bodies but also for large scale occasions of community realization and the recognition of the values for all contributed by many circles of life.

This antinomy of personal and societal religion has thus led us into a conception which may seem fantastic to some. It is a conception, however, which has already been sensed in a number of quarters. The dean of the cathedral of Saint John the Divine in New York City is making certain phases of the conception a reality. In Chicago there is a Free Cathedral Society organized to consider and foster the idea. It is a conception, moreover, which can guide experiments on a small scale in many places as a preliminary to more ambitious attempts. It is a conception which does not preclude but rather fosters any and all increased intensities of devotion in the line of specific and personal religion. It is a conception which grows inevitably out of any serious attempt to prefigure the possibilities of modern worship.

Amongst the problems of worship one of the most practical is that of congregational participation and priestly conduct. There is an increase of interest in what may be called democratic worship. There is a growing feeling which is wholesome and sound that social worship is something which must be genuinely shared by the individual worshipers, something to which each must contribute a vital part. The service of the Roman church is conducted entirely by the priest and choristers, the people having no share in the liturgy proper. But in the Roman church the people have been taught to make personal preparation for their devotions and to make active spiritual responses expressed by physical posture and gesture at appropriate points in the drama of the ritual. Though it seems to be slight, such participation is real and profound. The fault of the Protestant platform type of rhetorical sermon as the chief source of inspiration is just here. It is something done for the people rather than by them. It does not call forth previous preparation for worship nor worthy response and participation in the midst of worship. One of the difficulties which some ministers have discovered in their attempts to improve the service of worship is the unpreparedness of the people for their own necessary contribution to it. It is not wise to change customary forms too radically nor to set up a fixed form of liturgy which is planned for the minister only nor to arrange parts for the people which seem to them artificial. But it is possible with patience to develop liturgical parts such as short prayers, litany responses or creedal recitals in which the congregation can be led to participate in a genuine and simple manner. Sometimes modest improvements along these lines can be introduced without previous discussion. Sometimes the church itself can be interested in a desire for experiment and growth in the art of worship. In any case, it is necessary to avoid foisting upon the people strange usages which they cannot naturally share.

New modes of participation by the people will doubtless be discovered in new attempts to incorporate into the celebrations of religion the concerns of various social and civic circles of life. I know of no instance of an industrial group coming to church to present a kind of corporate offering of toil or a recital of accomplishments. The very attendance of an organized body to hear a recital made on their behalf would be a genuine mode of participation in public worship. The presence of persons representing several phases of industrial or civic life would afford opportunity for an increased sense of their common participation in larger ends than they severally achieve.

This brief notice of problems in contrast tends to confirm the value of the conception of worship as the celebration of life. And, in turn, the conception assists the solution of all the problems from that of good form to that of participation. Form is arrangement, design, order, categorical scheme. It is more than manners or method or other secondary concern. The great generic form of celebration will give order to the many concerns of a rich and varied content. Then in the experience of worship the integration of form will be transformed into the integration of purpose as the worshiper is moved to review the practical life and to return from celebration to toil. The adventure of worship is begun by retreat to the organizing and unifying form of the celebration of life in the sanctuary of God; it is not complete without the creative purpose of renewed participation in the practical life of the world.

Date Due

Date Due			
DEC 4 45			
Feb 5 46			
May 23 46			
DEC 20 46			
OCT 7 47			
MAY 5 '49			
MAY 6 '49			
MAR 24 50			
APR 19 '54			
NOV 5 '54			
JAN 2 2 1960			
MAR 1 6 1961			
FEB 2 3 1962			
MAR 18 '64			